*including*
- *Life and Background*
- *Introduction to* Emma
- *General Plot Summary*
- *List of Characters*
- *Chapter Summaries and Commentaries*
- *Critical Analysis*
- *Questions for Study and Review*
- *Selected Bibliography*

*by*
*Thomas J. Rountree, Ph.D.*
*University of Alabama*

**INCORPORATED**
LINCOLN, NEBRASKA  68501

Editor

Gary Carey, M.A.
University of Colorado

Consulting Editor

James L. Roberts, Ph.D.
Department of English
University of Nebraska

ISBN 0-8220-0434-8
© Copyright 1967
by
C. K. Hillegass
All Rights Reserved
Printed in U.S.A.

1989 Printing

Cliffs Notes, Inc.          Lincoln, Nebraska

# CONTENTS

# Emma

## LIFE AND BACKGROUND

While *Pride and Prejudice* is doubtless Jane Austen's most widely read and popular novel, many critics aver that her fullest achievement, the masterpiece of her six completed novels, is *Emma*. One cogent reason put forward is that at the time of its writing (January 21, 1814, to March 29, 1815) Miss Austen had reached a calm high point in her development as an artist, a point of steady, relaxed control over both her subject matter and her technique.

The temporal substance of her novels — the manners and interests of the upper middle class in late eighteenth- and early nineteenth-century England — was that of her own surroundings from the beginning. Born on December 16, 1775, the seventh of eight children — six boys and two girls — she had more than common varied contact with the limited world of provincial gentry because her father was a country clergyman, the rector of Steventon in the county of Hampshire in south-central England. Though she accompanied her elder sister Cassandra to two boarding schools only to return home at the age of nine to remain there, she had the advantage of growing up and studying in an educated family. In the evenings amid the needlework and other domestic activity, Mr. Austen read aloud. Some time was probably devoted to the utility of "improving conversation." In addition, the Austens were a novel-reading family. But for the novelist she was to become, her "education" was the total provincial community in which she came to maturity and of which she was to remain ever fond, as both a place to live and a scene to delineate. In a letter of her adulthood she said that "such a spot is the delight of my life; three or four families in a country village is the very thing to work on."

She knew and loved this life because, except for one real interval, she lived it; and it may be significant that during that extended interval she was unable to achieve any known completed work. This

**6**

eight-year period began in 1801 when Mr. Austen gave up the living of Steventon and retired to Bath. After his death in 1805 the mother and daughters moved to Southampton, where they remained until in 1809 they moved to the little town of Chawton. Before 1801, while Jane was still in her early twenties, she had written three unpublished novels: *Pride and Prejudice, Sense and Sensibility,* and *Northanger Abbey.* Upon removal to Chawton Cottage she began immediately to write again and, before her death on July 18, 1817, she completed, in order, *Mansfield Park, Emma,* and *Persuasion.* Beginning with the printing of *Sense and Sensibility* in 1811, each of the six novels was published, the new ones in short order after their completion, some of the works going into second and third, as well as French, editions by the time of her death.

Jane Austen loved the life around her. But she also saw it clearly enough to perceive its imperfections along with its perfections: an insight into the divided nature of things that was to set its imprint of cool liveliness upon every page that she wrote. She was aware, of course, of worldly happenings: the distant thunder of the American and French revolutions, the rise of Napoleon, the industrial revolution, the British maritime mutinies, the overdone peculiarities of Gothic and sentimental novels, the new emotional quality of Romanticism. But most of these historic fluxes did not come even as close as the blank margin of her pages. Instead, she concentrated upon eternal mixed qualities of humanity—of human relationships—exemplified in the provincial society about her. This life she knew intimately, and it was for her enough.

## INTRODUCTION TO *EMMA*

As has often been done, one can—and with truth—say that *Emma,* like Jane Austen's other novels, deals with the subject of young ladies finding proper husbands. On the surface this is what the story line of *Emma* is about, but the total subject matter of the book concerns much more than that. Within the chosen limits of upper-middle-class society and within the even more limited strict feminine point of view for telling the story (all the events are presented from within a domestic or social context, though not, as has been claimed, merely from within a drawing room), Miss Austen is fervently preoccupied with the way people behave. And this is the broad area of the moralist. If the moralist chooses, as Miss Austen does, to focus on the common rather than the exceptional behavior of people, he is more likely to write comedy than tragedy. If he is furthermore a serious moralist perceptive and understanding enough to keep a part—but only a part—of himself disengaged from the contradictory entanglements of his subject matter, his comedy has a good chance of being realized in terms of ironic satire.

The purpose of satire is to point a humorous finger at what is wrong, thereby indicating by implication what is right. Irony, as a method of achieving satire, makes use of contradictory, and some-times ambiguous, opposites. Throughout *Emma* a deeper theme than that of woman finding the appropriate man for herself pervades the action: Emma Woodhouse's story is a progression in self-deception. Having since childhood been obliged to manage her father, she still likes to manage things and, particularly, people. In fact, among her associates she feels confident to manage everyone except Mr. Knightley. In her long-term attempt to preside over the marriage-ability of Harriet Smith, the natural daughter of hitherto unknown persons, Emma pits herself against something in which she funda-mentally believes, the eighteenth-century belief in class status whereby one simply should stay in the class into which he is born. (She is also incidentally pitting herself against the process of natural selection of a mate.) She deludes herself that Harriet's parents *may* have been of importance and hence tries to marry her off to people above her station in life. With absolutely no foundation in fact, this delusion stems solely from Emma's willful imagination.

Mr. George Knightley, on the other hand, in his sedate and kindly way accepts the social status quo and governs himself ac-cordingly, even cautioning Emma about what she is doing. On this major thematic point, then, Emma represents imagination and Mr. Knightley stands for realistic reasoning (some would say merely realistic acceptance), two human characteristics that are so often in opposition that a contrasting pairing of them leads to irony. The story, of course, belongs primarily to Emma, for her willfulness most readily lends itself to satire and it is the feminine point of view that Jane Austen knows best. Still, for contrast, Mr. Knightley is often enough on the scene to keep us reminded of the other side of the coin, and Mr. Woodhouse, Emma's father, is constantly before us as an extreme example of one who wants to keep things the way they are. Of the two men, it is Mr. Woodhouse, so fearful of the least change that he bemoans the very thought of marriage and urges reason of health for not leaving his fireside even in good weather, who is the main object of satire on this side of the opposition.

What Miss Austen has done is to take two human traits and put them in different characters in order to make her contrast highly effective. They of course belong to human nature in general and represent those ironical mixed qualities of humanity and human relationships. Throughout the story a reader feels that somehow these extremes ideally should be able to meet on common ground and be resolved into something right. From her realistic point of departure as a storyteller, however, Miss Austen knows that relationships are tangential: hence the irony in the fact that the willfully imaginative Emma is the closest of blood relatives to the sedentary and senilely reasoning Mr. Woodhouse. There is doubtless significance far beyond the surface plotting of a love story in the fact that Miss Austen finally marries Emma and Mr. Knightley—that is, marries imagination and reason. Having realized her self-deception to some degree, Emma, with Mr. Knightley beside her, may now develop a proper balance within herself. Mr. Knightley, with Emma beside him, now seems to stand a good chance of never ending up on that dead-end street of static, senile reasoning at which Mr. Woodhouse has arrived. It is a common-ground marriage of reason and imagination, of head and heart, of common sense and goodness.

The ending of the story is, then, what we call a happy one. Or is it? In consideration of the bulk of the story about human foibles, Miss Austen gives us reason only for hope. She concludes the book with a final sentence about "the perfect happiness of the union." But this is said with at least a certain amount of tongue-in-cheek. Emma will not marry without her father's consent, and that comes only after the robbery of a nearby turkey house one night convinces Mr. Woodhouse that Mr. Knightley's living with them will be a needed protection. The close juxtaposition of this small causative event and the closing statement of the book connects the ridiculous with the more sublime and should at least make a reader wonder. Based on a moralistic realism as Miss Austen's satiric comedy is, it is not untypical of her in one twinkling to see both a robbed turkey house that will doubtless be replenished and a human household which, while it encloses a "perfect happiness of . . . union," also includes Mr. Woodhouse and the displacement of Mr. Knightley, who will now forego the ease and security of his own finer home, Donwell Abbey, in order to placate Emma and Mr. Woodhouse. Miss Austen's satire ends with an indication of what *might* be right; but she only points, for her moralistic realism will not let her be certain. She has seen too much of life for that. After all, who can say that Emma will never again try to manage things and people? In spite of robbers (and bridegrooms) this world is still full of turkeys, and Miss Austen knows that.

A brief word remains to be said about the ambiguity of opposites as Miss Austen sees them, and perhaps the best example is Emma's willful imagination, which stands in contrast to the reason of someone like Mr. Knightley. The ambiguity lies in a further contrast which embodies a contradiction. A lively imagination, in its purity, is an admirable and interesting quality. Perhaps willfulness, too, has its good points. But imagination can be too unfounded upon reality, and willfulness is perhaps too often misdirected because of its tendency to become presumptuous if not arrogant. Thus, on any one side of Miss Austen's oppositions there is ambiguity in that that side contains both good and bad inextricably fused. For this reason we can like and even admire Emma for the lively energy of her imagination, for her readiness to make amends, her benevolence, her affirmative sense of direction, while we are also critical of what she is doing.

Similarly we may feel that Mr. Knightley's reasoning does not make allowance for an adequate degree of imagination. Miss Bates's interminable talkativeness, which so comically places the petty and the significant on the same level, never includes a merciful consideration for the listener in spite of the fact that she is one of the kindest and best intentioned people who ever lived on or off a page. In Miss Austen's world (and who can prove that her world is not ours?) no good quality seems to be without some negative alloy. For this reason her satire not only probes the contradictory nature of opposite human qualities (contradictory because they are of one world and one humanity), but also considers the ambiguous mixture of good and bad in any one of these opposites.

Just as she never presents an actual emotional love scene (the one exception is found in *Emma* when Mr. Knightley declares the passion of his love to Emma) because her interest is in discovering the *effects* of emotion, she seems never to question *why* contradictions and ambiguities exist because she is basically a realist rather than a theorist. Rather than write of man and his relation to God or politics or abstract ideas, she wrote of human relationships. This may be why, in a letter to her nephew, she once referred to her fiction as "the little bit (two Inches wide) of Ivory on which I work with so fine a Brush, as produces little effect after much labour." Such a statement may, of course, be merely tongue-in-cheek modesty; but it is indicative of the fact that she deliberately limited her writing efforts not only to the provincial society which she knew and to the feminine point of view that was naturally hers but also to the mundane level of human behavior. Nonetheless, most readers of *Emma* find there the rich opacity, the delicacy, and the true polish of fine ivory, but few would agree that it is only two inches wide.

## GENERAL PLOT SUMMARY

### VOLUME ONE

Youthful Emma Woodhouse, whose long-time governess and friend Miss Taylor has just married Mr. Weston, takes some solace in being left alone with her aging father by claiming that she made the match herself. An old friend of the family, Mr. George Knightley, does not believe her, but in her certainty she decides that she must also marry off the young rector, Mr. Elton. Among her friends and acquaintances in the large and populous village of Highbury, she begins to notice young Harriet Smith, the pretty illegitimate seventeen-year-old who lives at Mrs. Goddard's boarding school.

Determining first to improve Harriet, Emma discourages her interest in worthy Robert Martin of Abbey-Mill Farm, declares that Harriet must be from more genteel parents than his, and fixes upon Harriet as Mr. Elton's future wife.

In bringing the two together socially, Emma does a drawing of Harriet which Mr. Elton admires and takes off to London to be framed. This appears so promising to Emma that, when Harriet receives a letter of proposal from Robert Martin, Emma discredits him and actually helps Harriet write a letter of refusal in spite of the fact that Mr. Knightley has nothing but respect for Robert. Ensuing events convince Emma that Harriet and Mr. Elton are developing a mutual regard, and she takes pride in the apparent success of her endeavor, at the same time affirming that she herself will never marry.

For the Christmas holidays Mr. and Mrs. John Knightley, respectively the brother of George Knightley and the sister of Emma, come from London with their five children to visit the Woodhouses. On December 24, which proves to be a bad day of snow, all of them, including George Knightley and Mr. Elton, go for a dinner with the Westons. There discussion turns to Frank Churchill, Weston's handsome, polished son by a former marriage (Frank had taken his uncle's name upon going to live with him) but a son who has never been seen in Highbury. John Knightley in particular thinks it oddly improper that Frank has not yet called on his newly remarried father, even though Frank lives some distance away in Yorkshire with the Churchills. There have been letters from him, of course, and a pleasant surprise of the dinner party is an announcement that a recent letter says that Frank will be coming for a visit within a fortnight, an announcement that reminds Emma that, if she *were* ever to marry, Frank would suit her in age, character, and condition.

The snow increases to the point that the visitors feel that they must go if they are to reach home safely. To her consternation Emma finds herself alone with Mr. Elton in the second carriage. But she is disconcerted even more when he begins insistently to declare his love for her and when he is amazed to learn that she thought him in love with Harriet. Emma's refusal of Mr. Elton's offer is firm, but she is indeed worried that he has never thought seriously of Harriet. Her worry and self-criticism continue through the night, mixed with resentment at the impertinence of Mr. Elton's aspirations toward herself. Fortunately for her, during the next few days everyone is confined to home by the weather. On the first good day, the John Knightleys return to London while Mr. Elton informs Mr. Woodhouse in a note that he is leaving for a visit to Bath. It is Emma's unhappy duty to inform Harriet about Mr. Elton and to console her, inwardly blaming herself for being in error. In addition to this disappointment in her plans, she learns that Frank Churchill has once again had to defer his visit because Mrs. Churchill is ill, a condition that many of Highbury doubt. George Knightley in particular questions Frank's real sense of duty toward Mr. Weston and, in a conversation with Emma, indicates that he does not share Highbury's (and Emma's) general tendency to think highly of the young man whom the town has never yet seen.

## VOLUME TWO

Though Miss Bates, as a harmless but compulsive talker, is disagreeable in Emma's eyes, Emma pays a duty call to her and Mrs. Bates and learns that Miss Bates's orphan niece Jane Fairfax will arrive next week for a two-months visit. Jane upon arrival is elegant, accomplished, and reserved, and Emma does not like her —likes her even less, in fact, when she learns that Jane and Frank Churchill had met at Weymouth.

George Knightley is about to tell Emma some news when Miss Bates and Jane arrive to announce that Mr. Elton, still in Bath, has become engaged to Augusta Hawkins there. Later Harriet comes to say that she has encountered Robert Martin and his sister at Ford's shop downtown, but Emma takes her mind off it by relating the news about Mr. Elton.

Frank Churchill finally arrives and is very agreeable and lively. From the time of his first visit to the Woodhouses, it is evident that Mr. and Mrs. Weston would like to make a match between him and Emma; but the call is ended by his going off to see the Bateses and Jane Fairfax. On subsequent meetings Emma is won over by

Frank, and in their discussion of Jane and her reserve Frank perfectly agrees with Emma. Faith in him is shaken when he runs off to London just to get a haircut, but he returns unabashed and continues to sparkle. At a party given by the Coles, Frank sits attentively beside Emma. Jane, it is learned, has received a new pianoforte. When Emma hints that Mr. Dixon, the husband of Jane's friend in Ireland, sent it, Frank politely agrees. Because of some impromptu dancing at the Coles, Emma and Frank later plan a dance at the Crown Inn, but everything is overthrown when Frank has to leave owing to Mrs. Churchill's illness. Before going, Frank visits the Bateses and then the Woodhouses, leaving Emma pretty well convinced that he is in love with her, though she can picture herself only as refusing him.

Emma now thinks she is in love with Frank, but his letters to Mrs. Weston make Emma think also that she can do without him. Meanwhile her attention is taken up with Harriet and the arrival of Mrs. Augusta Elton, who has ease without elegance, is vain and overly talkative, and proves to be an insufferable organizer and "manager." Mr. Knightley shows such respect for Jane Fairfax that Emma thinks he may be falling in love, but he declares that he would never ask her to marry him.

At a dinner which Emma dutifully gives for the Eltons, Jane discloses that she always fetches the mail from the post office, and Mrs. Elton insists upon coming to her general relief by finding a situation as governess for her. But Jane, who is now to stay longer with the Bateses than originally intended, says that she does not wish anything attempted at the present. In the midst of things, Mr. Weston arrives with the news that Frank will be with them again soon because on doctor's orders Mrs. Churchill must come to London for a stay in May.

## VOLUME THREE

By the time Frank Churchill returns, Emma realizes that there is no attachment on her part. The ball at the Crown Inn now takes place. When Harriet proves to have no dancing partner and Mr. Elton obviously slights her, George Knightley, who has not danced before, gallantly leads her to the set and afterward even dances with Emma.

The next day Frank rescues Harriet from some gypsies, and Emma thinks she sees something developing between them but decides not to interfere: it will be a mere passive scheme. Harriet indicates that she is interested in someone above her, and Emma is sure that it is Frank. During a gathering at which they play a word game, Frank shoves words at Jane which make George Knightley suspect that the two are involved, but Emma will not believe him.

In June a strawberry party is held at Donwell Abbey, George Knightley's estate. Emma observes George and Harriet walking together. Frank does not arrive; Jane Fairfax leaves early to walk home; and finally Frank arrives in agitation, not at all his usual smooth self. The next day on an exploring party to Box Hill, Emma and Frank flirt; Jane appears bothered; and Emma is rude to Miss Bates. When Emma goes to make amends the next morning, she learns that Jane has accepted a position as governess and will be leaving soon. Frank too has to leave, but immediately, for Mrs. Churchill is ill and, in fact, soon dies. Emma feels sorry for Jane's having to take a position, but her attentions are repulsed.

Ten days later the Westons receive a brief letter from Frank in which he explains that he and Jane have been engaged since their being together at Weymouth; Mr. Churchill now gives his consent. It turns out that Harriet has not been thinking of Frank at all but rather of George Knightley. When Emma learns this, she is awakened to the fact that Mr. Knightley must marry no one but herself and she wishes that she had never seen Harriet and had let her marry Robert Martin. Knightley returns from a business trip, learns the news, and commiserates with Emma, who assures him that she has never been captivated by Frank. The revelation leads Knightley to declare his own feelings for Emma, and they become engaged, though Emma knows that they cannot marry as long as she has to take care of her father, for she cannot leave him and he will not leave his home.

A very reasonable letter from Frank to Mrs. Weston explains satisfactorily his conduct at Highbury and his and Jane's need for secrecy. Emma is relieved, but she cannot set her mind at rest about Harriet, who now goes to visit the John Knightleys in London. Emma and Jane become reconciled as friends; George Knightley decides that, since Emma cannot leave her father, he will live with them; then it takes the combined persuasive forces of Emma, Knightley, and the Westons to get Mr. Woodhouse to agree to the marriage. When Harriet decides to marry Robert Martin after all, Emma feels free enough that, after some small delaying tactics by Mr. Woodhouse, she and George Knightley are wed in "perfect happiness."

# LIST OF CHARACTERS

## Emma Woodhouse

The imaginative and self-deceived heroine of the novel. At almost twenty-one years of age, she is handsome, accomplished, and willful, her main duty in life that of being companion and mistress of the house for her widower father.

## Henry Woodhouse

Emma's elderly father, who basks in routine and Emma's attentions and resists any kind of change, compensating somewhat for his selfish whims by being kindly and concerned about people's health.

## George Knightley

A well-to-do man of about thirty-seven or thirty-eight, an admirably calm and rational man who for years has befriended and advised Emma.

## Miss Anne Taylor

For years Emma's devoted governess and friend, who at the beginning of the novel has just married Mr. Weston.

### Mr. Weston

A near neighbor to the Woodhouses, whose son by a former marriage is Frank Churchill.

### Philip Elton

The rector of Highbury, a twenty-six-year-old clergyman who is very eligible for marriage.

### Frank Churchill

Mr. Weston's son, who has never visited Highbury but who has a reputation for polished charm and manners.

### Miss Hetty Bates

The kindly old maid talker who, at least in her dialogue, runs the details of everything together as of equal importance.

### Jane Fairfax

Miss Bates's orphan niece, elegant and accomplished, who has visited her aunt in Highbury before but not for two years now.

### Harriet Smith

The illegitimate, seventeen-year-old girl whom Emma befriends and tries to marry off to Mr. Elton.

### Robert Martin

A respected young farmer who wants to marry Harriet Smith.

### Augusta Hawkins

A vain and talkative young lady whom Mr. Elton meets on a trip to Bath and to whom he quickly gets himself engaged.

### John and Isabella Knightley

Respectively the brother of George Knightley and the sister of Emma Woodhouse, they, except for occasional visits to Highbury, live in London with their five children.

### Mrs. Goddard

The lady who runs the boarding school where Harriet Smith lives.

### Mr. and Mrs. Cole

A *nouveau riche* couple who are determinedly making their way into Highbury society.

### Mr. Perry

The village apothecary, who is Mr. Woodhouse's constant reference on matters of health.

# Summaries and Commentaries

## VOLUME ONE

### CHAPTER I

#### Summary

In the town of Highbury Emma Woodhouse, a handsome, clever, and rich young lady of twenty-one, is left alone with her indulgent widower father by the marriage of Miss Taylor, her governess and friend of sixteen years, to Mr. Weston. Emma's older sister Isabella is married to John Knightley, and the Knightleys live sixteen miles away in London with their five children.

At teatime the day after the marriage, Mr. Woodhouse, who has been a valetudinarian all his life and is against any kind of change, speaks of "Poor Miss Taylor!"—not because of Mr. Weston, who is a fine and wealthy man, but simply because of the fact of marriage. Emma is trying to appease him when George Knightley, John's brother, a sensible and quite wealthy man of about thirty-seven or thirty-eight who lives at his Donwell Abbey estate a mile from the Woodhouse estate of Hartfield, pays them a cheerful visit.

When Emma states that she herself made the match between Miss Taylor and Mr. Weston, George says that she only guessed that it would come and Mr. Woodhouse asks her not to make any more. Emma's reply is that she will make only one more—for Mr. Elton, the twenty-six-year-old rector—to which George answers that she should "leave him to chuse his own wife."

## Commentary

In this chapter Jane Austen begins to set up the situation from which the story line of the novel is to come, and she does this primarily through the characterization of Emma. For the first time in her life, Emma is left to herself and her own devices. Whereas before she has always had at least one close companion, she now has only her father, and he is a lovingly accepted burden rather than a companion. No longer having a confidante, she relies upon her imagination, first realizing that she *could* have made the match between Miss Taylor and Mr. Weston and then stating that she did do it. George Knightley's reasonable exception to this comes as a kind of challenge that stimulates Emma's willfulness, so that she declares not only that she will make another match but who the man will be.

As a preparatory scene this chapter also sets up the opposition between imagination and reasoning, both ironically based upon realism: people do find their own mates, but likewise matches are sometimes made by third parties. Furthermore, though it is done very unobtrusively, Austen places before the reader two characters who are quite eligible for marriage: Emma and George. Equally unobtrusive is the idea of properly established social ranks. The author is careful to make Miss Taylor and Mr. Weston relatively equal in character and social standing. The short talk between Emma and her father about servants, while it confirms Mr. Woodhouse's kindness to others, also fixes the idea of a definite servant class which one enters by birth and remains in as an accepted and honorable position.

In general the chapter presents a provincial situation of established order, an order mocked slightly by the presentation of Mr. Woodhouse's exaggerated conservatism. It is an order of intimates and manners and routine, where nothing more drastic than a marriage or an unreturned call is likely to happen. It is, so to speak, a world of its own. And it is about to be threatened by change because a bright young lady has been left in "intellectual solitude." Part of the irony is that a normal social and human act (Miss Taylor's marriage) within this order leads to the disruptive element (Emma's solitary imagination). Another part of the irony will be that, after the undue human concern over the disruption, nothing in the order of things will have been changed after all. Only the aberrant Emma will change.

# CHAPTER II

## Summary

Mr. Weston, a Highbury native of respectable family, was formerly a captain in the militia, a life that led him to meet and marry Miss Churchill of a great Yorkshire family. When she died three years later, their one child Frank went to live with the Churchills and took their family name. Mr. Weston then engaged successfully in trade for the next eighteen or twenty years, finally buying and settling at Randalls, a property near Highbury which he had long wanted. Never an unhappy man, he is thus situated when he marries Miss Taylor.

Though one of the boasts of Highbury, Frank Churchill has never been there. Now, however, gossip and speculation about his coming are strengthened by a "handsome letter" from him to Mrs. Weston. Whenever the latter visits the Woodhouses, Mr. Woodhouse invariably sighs, "Ah! poor Miss Taylor. She would be very glad to stay." This, of course, is not the case; it is merely symptomatic of a man who can "never believe other people to be different from himself." Similarly, he had earlier been so distressed about the wedding cake that he had consulted the indulgent apothecary Mr. Perry, who agreed that wedding cake certainly might disagree with many. Nonetheless there is a "strange rumor" that all of the Perry children ate of the cake.

### Commentary

Much of this short chapter is plain exposition, preparatory material which "places" Mr. Weston and points to Frank, who will later figure prominently in the story. In addition, the chapter assures us of the happy appropriateness of the Weston marriage and indicates the satiric potential of the low-key interests of the provincial community: its people's intimate concern with each others' affairs and its easy tolerance of Mr. Woodhouse's gentle selfishness.

## CHAPTERS III-IV

### Summary

Mr. Woodhouse is fond of society among his intimates who "visit him on his own terms," especially for evening parties: George Knightley, the Westons, Mr. Elton, Mrs. Goddard, and Mrs. and Miss Bates. A happy woman, Miss Bates is known for her "universal good-will and contented temper" and for being "a great talker upon little matters." Mrs. Goddard runs an honest, old-fashioned, and respectable boarding school; and she delights Emma when she asks to be allowed one evening to bring Harriet Smith, a pretty seventeen-year-old who is "the natural daughter of somebody." After Harriet proves to be engaging, proper, and deferential, Emma decides to "improve her" and spends a pleasant evening in forming schemes for doing so, at the same time seeing that the guests get generous portions of food, in spite of Mr. Woodhouse's concern that they partake of only a little because of health. The evening ends with Harriet in absolute happiness at the attention she has received from "so great a personage in Highbury" as Miss Woodhouse.

Harriet becomes such a good walking companion that Emma is confirmed in her kind designs, recognizing that, though Harriet is not clever, she is sweet and grateful and needs only guidance. Unable to learn from Harriet who her parents are, since she does not know, Emma encourages her to talk and learns that she is well acquainted with the Martins of Abbey-Mill Farm, where she had spent two months. From what Harriet says, Emma is sure that Mrs. Martin is successfully trying to interest Harriet in her son Robert. Emma's tactic is to say that she is sure that Harriet would not take notice of anyone Robert would marry, one reason being that there is "no doubt of your being a gentleman's daughter."

When they accidentally meet Robert the next day, Harriet steps over to talk with him and Emma observes him for a distance. He looks both neat and sensible, but shortly afterward Emma remarks that he is plain and entirely lacking in gentility and leads Harriet to compare him unfavorably with George Knightley, Mr. Weston, and Mr. Elton, particularly the latter. Whereas Robert reads little and lets business make him forget to procure a book that Harriet has recommended, Mr. Elton (according to Emma) is educated, has superior manners, and is in fine a model for any young man. After such an encomium Emma repeats some warm personal praise of Harriet which Emma herself has drawn from Mr. Elton. Emma has, of course, fixed upon Harriet as Mr. Elton's future mate, deluding herself that others must have already seen it as a perfect match but that only she could have planned it so precisely.

*Commentary*

In these chapters the self-deception of Emma takes positive shape and unfortunately involves others. She, like others around her, obviously believes in the propriety of social stratification and exemplifies it when she leads the believing Harriet to compare

Robert Martin with the other *gentlemen*. However, it is worth remembering that when Emma says, "The yeomanry are precisely the order of people with whom I feel I can have nothing to do," she is not being snobbish in the modern sense. Though it may not be admirable by today's standards, her social conscience is that of the eighteenth century; and it is significant that her very next remarks, coming without pause, are these: "A degree or two lower and a creditable appearance might interest me; I might hope to be useful to their families in some way or other. But a farmer can need none of my help, and is therefore in one sense as much above my notice as in every other he is below it." In light of the world around her, Emma's only serious mistake, socially and humanly speaking, is in letting her willful wish and imagination convince her that Harriet, who is so pretty and amiable, must come from gentility.

In the first of these two chapters, Miss Austen introduces the reader to two important new characters, Harriet and Miss Bates. Harriet will be a mere pretty counter to be maneuvered by Emma and the plot of the novel, but Miss Bates is to be the object of ruthlessly gentle satire and, through her relation to Jane Fairfax (introduced later), an important sideline element in the total plot of the novel. Mr. Elton's future use for satire is indicated in the present description of him as "a young man living alone without liking it."

## CHAPTER V

### Summary

George Knightley and Mrs. Weston have a discussion—a near argument, in fact—about Emma's relation with Harriet. George is convinced that nothing good can come of it for either party. When Mrs. Weston says it will lead to Emma's reading more, his short reply is that "Emma has been meaning to read more ever since she was twelve years old" and that she will never subject "the fancy to the understanding." After he refers ironically to "Emma's genius for foretelling and guessing," Mrs. Weston shifts the talk to Emma's beauty, eliciting from him the statement that "I love to look at her" and that Emma's vanity lies another way than personal appearance. Mrs. Weston can see no wrong in Emma and requests and advises

George not to make an issue of the friendship between Emma and Harriet. George agrees and, in wondering what will become of Emma, recalls, "She always declares she will never marry." Mrs. Weston's reply is a vague one that hides some wishes that the Westons have respecting Emma's destiny.

## Commentary

The picture of George Knightley here is that of a realist. He is a man of understanding or reason, and he is quite right about Emma but too amiable really to interpose. His statement about Emma's not reading books is ironical when we recall Emma's recent criticism of Robert Martin for the very same neglect. In stating his view of what a wife should be, George refers to Mrs. Weston's talent for submission of her will; and yet by the end of the chapter it is George himself who has submitted to her. (Note: in the novel he is always called Mr. Knightley; his first name is presently used to distinguish him from his brother John.)

The delineation of Mrs. Weston in this chapter helps to explain why Emma is as she is, for, as always, Mrs. Weston has absolute innocent faith in her former ward. Her hinted wishes that they at Randalls have for Emma constitute the author's preparation for further plot complications.

### CHAPTER VI

## Summary

Emma is pleased with her development of Harriet, especially in the latter's progressing sensibility toward Mr. Elton. She feels likewise that there is some success in regard to Mr. Elton, who has perceived "the striking improvement of Harriet's manner." With his eager agreement, Emma proposes to do a drawing of Harriet. Emma plays and sings well and has done various portraits without ever finishing any of them, for "steadiness had always been wanting." Nonetheless, her style is spirited, and the sitting begins with Mr.

Elton fidgeting behind Emma until she has him read to them. With the picture completed, others find some small faults in it; but Mr. Elton is determined to find everything in it exactly right almost to the point of perfection. When it is decided that all the portrait lacks is being framed and that that must be done in London, Mr. Elton gladly takes on the project. Emma thinks that he is being almost too gallant to be in love but decides that it is only his way. She realizes that, while doing the picture, she has been the object of many of his compliments; but she assures herself that it is merely "his gratitude on Harriet's account."

### Commentary

Mr. Elton is portrayed as determined to be almost simperingly pleasing—a character ripe for satire. But the emphasis in this section is on Emma's self-deception. More than ever convinced that she is rightly succeeding with Harriet, she is too intent to see that all of Mr. Elton's compliments could have been aimed at her and that, for a rector or just an honest man, he comes very close to being sycophantic. Her intensity is further demonstrated in that for the first time in her life she is able to complete a portrait. In a moment of willfulness she finds the steadiness which she has formerly lacked, but this steadiness is founded upon a misdirected imagination.

## CHAPTER VII

### Summary

On the very day of Mr. Elton's going to London, Harriet receives a letter with a direct proposal of marriage from Robert Martin. When shown it, Emma admits that it is a well-written letter but plants doubt in Harriet's mind. When Harriet asks her point-blank what she should do, Emma backs off a bit but not enough but what she is really directing Harriet every minute. After Harriet commits herself to rejecting Robert, Emma congratulates her and suggests that Harriet write her refusal to him. And while "Emma continued to protest against any assistance being wanted, it was in fact given in the formation of every sentence." Afterward Emma manages to distract her by talking about Mr. Elton and the portrait he is taking to London.

## Commentary

This scene demonstrates the degree of control Emma has gained over pretty, unreasoning Harriet as well as her finesse in making Harriet believe that the decision is her own. For Harriet quite naturally is drawn toward Robert. After Harriet has made up her mind to reject him, Emma is heartless enough to say, "It would have grieved me to lose your acquaintance, which must have been the consequence of your marrying Mr. Martin." In light of her strong wishes, Emma may feel herself justified in saying this, but it is nonetheless a genuine dagger thrust of cruelty, hardly to be excused by anyone except a Harriet Smith. Emma, it appears, will go far to have her way.

## CHAPTER VIII

### Summary

Since Harriet now has a bedroom at the Woodhouses, she sleeps at Hartfield this night. The next morning, while she is away at Mrs. Goddard's, George Knightley calls and talks with Emma. He voluntarily discusses Harriet, thinking that he sees improvement in her; then he indicates that Harriet can expect a proposal from Robert Martin, who has consulted George and whom George praises strongly for his good qualities. When Emma reveals that Robert has already written and been refused, George is indignant and accuses Emma of misleading Harriet into pretension and false hope. He guesses that Mr. Elton is the object of Emma's intrigue and assures her that it will not work. Emma thanks him for his advice and he leaves abruptly. When Harriet returns, she talks of nothing but Mr. Elton, who, she has learned, is "actually on his road to London" with the portrait.

### Commentary

George is further characterized as a strong and sensible man of reason. He grants that Emma too has reason but he cautions her plainly about it: "Better be without sense, than misapply it as you do." His recommendation of Robert for Harriet comes from his recognition and acceptance of social classification, despite the fact that, in direct opposition to Emma's guesses and hopes, he suggests that Harriet's parentage may well be very inferior to Robert's. On the other hand, Emma is saved from a one-sided, willful character-ization by the indication that, in reference to George, she has "habit-ual respect for his judgment in general"; she nonetheless will not agree with him on this particular subject of Harriet.

## CHAPTERS IX-X

### Summary

The framed portrait arrives, and Emma turns to improving Harriet further. It is, however, easier to chat than read, and so they turn to the only "literary" pursuit interesting to Harriet: riddles, which she starts collecting in a book. Mr. Elton is persuaded to com-pose a charade, which he brings over the next morning, saying that it is a friend's. After he leaves, Harriet cannot fathom its meaning, but Emma immediately sees that the solution is the word *courtship*. Emma is so delighted at her apparent success that, in spite of Mr. Elton's earlier wishes to the contrary, she copies the poem in Har-riet's book, an act that disconcerts Mr. Elton when he returns and learns of it, though he takes it gallantly.

Walking the next morning on a charitable visit to a poor sick family, Emma answers a question from Harriet by declaring the improbabilities of *her* ever marrying. Harriet is struck with femi-nine horror at the possibility of her friend's being an old maid, like Miss Bates. Emma assures her that she will always have nieces around her but that she will never harp about them as Miss Bates does about Jane Fairfax, a subject that tires Emma because Miss Bates is so tiresome a talker.

After rendering their genuinely kind services to the sick family, the two young ladies are returning home when they meet Mr. Elton on a visit to the same family. Eager to give the two "lovers" a chance, Emma deliberately separates herself from them after Mr. Elton postpones his visit to escort them. She further delays with a supposedly broken shoelace, then breaks it in order to gain entrance to the nearby vicarage, the interior of which Harriet has never seen. Contriving to leave the other two alone, Emma goes into a back room with the housekeeper. Ten minutes later she returns to the gratifying sight of them talking near the window. Still, Mr. Elton has not come to the point with Harriet, and Emma disappointedly credits him with being cautious, "very cautious." Determined to be optimistic, she flatters herself that the incident is a step forward "to the great event."

*Commentary*

These pages intensify Emma's self-deception. She is more than ever determined to read every act by Mr. Elton as a growing interest in Harriet—so determined that she misinterprets and is disappointed, even irritated, at the lack of ultimate results, though she can still draw optimistic conclusions. Her willfulness and stratagems stand in contrast to her genuine and realistic kindness in other matters such as the poor sick family.

In addition, Harriet's utter simplicity is exemplified; Mr. Elton's increasing gallantry and interest are made at least ambiguous to the reader if not to Emma; and Jane Fairfax is mentioned to prepare for her later appearance in the novel as a foil for Emma.

## CHAPTERS XI-XII

*Summary*

The John Knightleys arrive from London with their five children for the Christmas vacation with the Woodhouses. Isabella is in interests very much like her father, except that her disposition is a little more amiable and her concerns over matters of health have a more varied outlet; she submits absolutely to her father and her lawyer husband. John, on the other hand, is more like his brother George, except that at times he is less gentle and circumspect with his frank criticism; he lacks some of George's respectful forbearance toward Mr. Woodhouse. Talk naturally turns to Mrs. Weston, over whom Mr. Woodhouse continues his unwarranted lamentations. John sees the real happiness of Mrs. Weston's situation but refrains from correcting Mr. Woodhouse, much to Emma's relief. Instead he inquires about Frank Churchill, wondering that the twenty-three-year-old son has not visited his father since the marriage. When he criticizes Mr. Weston for his easy-going giving up of his son and for enjoying society more than family, Emma almost challenges him in defense of Mr. Weston; but she forbears because she senses something honorable and valuable in John's strong domestic habits, his commitment to family: "It had a high claim to forbearance."

That evening George Knightley is to dine with them. In order to help make up with him about their argument, Emma, with good calculation, has her eight-month-old niece Emma in her arms when he arrives. He is mollified but comments that, if she "were as much guided by nature" in estimating men and women as she is with children, the two of them might always think alike. Afterward the evening is quiet and convivial for everyone. Still, primarily because of Mr. Woodhouse, every conversational subject leads back to matters of sickness or health, and Mr. Woodhouse laments that the John Knightleys' last vacation was spent at the seaside. With constant recurrence to Mr. Perry's recommendations (which are really Mr. Woodhouse's own), he finally provokes John to say that Mr. Perry "would do as well to keep his opinion till it is asked for." George comes to the rescue of the situation by changing the subject, but it requires "the soothing attentions of his daughters" to remove for Mr. Woodhouse "the present evil."

## Commentary

Perhaps better than any other section of the novel, these chapters demonstrate the domestic atmosphere of the book: the family and its interrelated contact with the rest of society as the foundation for the provincial community which Miss Austen is delineating and satirizing. It is important to note that Emma too accepts this governing concept, for this underlies the constant concern with the process and propriety of courtship and marriage. Even Mr. Woodhouse's trivially perpetual anxiety about health is part of it. And such a foundation is as natural as Emma's reaction, which George observes, toward children.

It is nonetheless worth noting that Emma *uses* this natural reaction in order to mollify George and gain her way. Emma is as much Emma as ever, but the authorial presentation of the opposite, conservative side of the contrast is doubled by the introduction of Isabella as being much like her father and of John as being much like George. The conflictive variety within the domestic setting is intensified.

## CHAPTER XIII

*Summary*

The visit of the John Knightleys is a delightful one, with casual visiting in the neighborhood; but one event calls for persuading Mr. Woodhouse: they must all dine at Randalls on the day before Christmas. The dinner is to include Harriet, Mr. Elton, and George Knightley; but Harriet goes back to Mrs. Goddard's with a cold that develops into a bad sore throat. After a visit to her bedridden friend, Emma encounters first Mr. Elton and then John Knightley. When Mr. Elton asks Emma not to run risks by visiting the sick one, she in turn insists that he do likewise, thereby hoping he will not attend the dinner but rather, being at home, inquire after Harriet every hour. This scheme is spoiled when John offers to take Mr. Elton to the dinner in his carriage.

Left alone with John, Emma is vexed and then amused when John suggests strongly that Mr. Elton is interested in her and that she has perhaps encouraged him. She assures him that they "are very good friends, and nothing more."

On the twenty-fourth the cold is severe and a few flakes of snow are falling. In the carriage John complains about people's insisting upon visits, but Emma refrains from answering him. After they pick up Mr. Elton, Emma is the first to mention Harriet and is surprised at how quickly Mr. Elton can move to other subjects; she is, in fact, astonished at his spirits. When he anticipates the coming dinner party, John's only anticipation is getting through the evening and then finding himself safely—and comfortably—back at Hartfield.

*Commentary*

Miss Austen is neatly building toward the climax of Volume One. In a quite natural way she removes Harriet from the upcoming scene, a social gathering equally natural to human beings, though the irony of man's thorough commitment to socializing is indicated in John Knightley's grumbling (as the carriage proceeds through the cold and snow) about their "setting forward voluntarily, without excuse, in defiance of the voice of nature." Emma is given what seems to be plenty of warning about Mr. Elton both by John's cautioning her and by Mr. Elton's blithe and solicitous conversation in the carriage and his ready forgetfulness of Harriet. But Emma is blinded by her willful scheming. Ironically, her reaction to John is to think confidently "of the blunders which often arise from a partial knowledge of circumstances, of the mistakes which people of high pretensions to judgment are for ever falling into," never for a moment applying these thoughts to herself. As for Mr. Elton, she is at the moment merely astonished at him—and critical.

## CHAPTER XIV

*Summary*

Upon their arrival at the Westons' home, Emma's tendency toward enjoyment asserts itself and she determines to think "as little as possible of Mr. Elton's oddities." But he compounds her vexation by placing himself close to her at the first opportunity, and for the first time Emma wonders if John could have been right, if Mr. Elton could be "beginning to transfer his affections from Harriet" to her—an "absurd" idea.

Because of his attentions, she cannot overhear another interesting group conversation; but at dinner, happily released to sit beside Mr. Weston, she learns that Frank Churchill is expected for a visit about the second week in January. Emma is still resolved never to marry, but she has frequently thought "that if she *were* to marry, he was the very person to suit her in age, character and condition." It is only a thought, however, for she would not give up her present situation for anything. After dinner, with the ladies retired to the drawing room, Mrs. Weston confirms the news about Frank and voices her doubts about it. She does not want to be unduly critical but she has heard of Mrs. Churchill's variable and demanding temper, and even Isabella agrees about the character of that lady. Emma is critical of Frank and his delayed visit, but Mrs. Weston tries to defend him. Knowing of his repeated excuses, Emma coolly replies, "I shall not be satisfied, unless he comes."

*Commentary*

In terms of plot movement, this chapter does two primary things. It advances the strand involving Mr. Elton, showing more and more to the reader, if not to Emma, what the vicar is up to. In addition it focuses attention more fully than ever upon Frank Churchill, who will enter the story in person in Volume Two and be a main character in the rest of the novel. For the reader, as for the people of Highbury, his character is in doubt; and doubt is calculated to arouse anticipation and expectant interest.

A curious honesty in Emma's self-deception also is given in this chapter. Beginning to wonder about John's statements and Mr. Elton's actions, she can conceive only that Mr. Elton may be starting to *transfer* his affections from Harriet to herself—not that she has been the object all along. This is, of course, the honesty of obduracy. Interestingly and tantalizingly enough, Emma, ever connected with the theme of marriage, can conceive of Frank as possibly a suitable partner for her even as, in the same mental breath, she reaffirms her resolution of never marrying. These thoughts of hers are also part of the plot movement calculated to foster the reader's expectant interest.

## CHAPTER XV

*Summary*

When the gentlemen join the ladies in the drawing room, Mr. Elton immediately seats himself on the sofa between Emma and Mrs. Weston and becomes so vocally anxious about Emma's escaping the throat infection that, in her vexation, she admits that his entreaties appear "exactly like the pretence of being in love with her, instead of Harriet."

John comes in with the information that snow now covers the ground and more is coming fast. This naturally upsets poor Mr. Woodhouse, and everyone wonders what must be done. Always sensible and practical, George, who has slipped out to investigate, returns to say that nowhere is the snow more than half an inch deep and that travel will be easy for at least another hour. He and Emma quickly settle the question and order the carriages brought around. To her further vexation Emma finds herself alone in the second carriage with Mr. Elton.

The three-quarter-mile trip is hardly begun when the vicar seizes her hand and declares his adoring love and need of her, "ready to die" if she refuses him. When she deliberately but delicately brings up the name of Harriet, he is amazed but resumes his own passion, "urgent for a favourable answer." Struck by his inconstancy and presumption, she accuses him of misbehavior toward Harriet, whereupon he says, "I never thought of Miss Smith in the whole course of my existence — never paid her any attentions, but as your friend." Pressing his point, he makes clear that he thinks Harriet is beneath him and declares that he has received encouragement from Emma herself. Emma denies this, upbraids him for his attitude toward Harriet, and flatly states, "I have no thoughts of matrimony at present." The rest of the trip is spent in angry silence. After leaving him at the vicarage, the carriage takes her to Hartfield, where she finds everyone in peace and comfort — everyone except herself.

## Commentary

The action of this chapter is the external climax of Volume One, and the action speaks pretty much for itself. The fiasco of a proposal is in contrast to the comfortable domesticity all around it; and as a real emotional mishap on the return trip home, it stands out in ironic relief against the earlier apprehensions of physical misadventure on the snow-covered road.

The concluding incident of the chapter marks the beginning of revelation and self-revelation for Emma. The situation constitutes a point of extreme testing of an imaginative young lady, and in spite of a hesitant moment or two, she meets the event with superb outward control. It is also worth noting that her conviction of his "presumption" comes, if we are to judge from her total reactions to him up to this point in the story, as much from a sense of incompatibility as from a sense of social levels, though she would probably feel that the two are inseparable.

CHAPTER XVI

*Summary*

Emma is ready for bed, her hair curled and the maid sent away. She can now evaluate the evening's events and consider "the evil to Harriet." She wonders "How she could have been so deceived!" and reviews all the events in connection with Harriet, including the earlier caution that George Knightley had given. Concluding that Mr. Elton has no real affection for herself and wants only to enrich himself through her as an heiress of thirty thousand pounds, she is obliged in honesty to admit that her complaisance, courtesy, and attention might have led him to misunderstand her. Granting that the first and worst error lay at her door, she is ashamed and resolves "to do such things no more." She turns her thoughts to Harriet again and within a moment wonders about soothing her friend's disappointment by making William Coxe the object of new intrigue, but he is an unendurable, pert young lawyer. Blushing and laughing at her own relapse, Emma goes to bed with nothing settled.

The next morning she is more disposed for comfort, especially when the sight of much snow on the ground informs her that she, Harriet, and Mr. Elton will be kept "quite asunder at present." In fact, though it is Christmas Day, she cannot get to church. Because of further snow and freezes, the confinement extends for days and only George Knightley, "whom no weather could keep entirely from them," ventures outdoors. Since John is cleared of the ill humor which he had at Randalls, having her sister's family in the house is a matter of pure pleasure for Emma—or would be if the coming explanation with Harriet did not hang over her like an evil thing.

*Commentary*

Whereas the preceding chapter encompassed the external, physical climax of Volume One, this chapter presents the internal climax. With outward events making Emma's blindness to them no longer possible, she must adjust and come to terms as much as she can with the realities of the situation. This means that she must admit and come to terms with her own self-deception. Since she is an intelligent and sympathetic heroine, it is only right that she be as fair as possible—and she is. She accepts her own errors and, in regard to Harriet at least, she plans to face the issue and do what she can to improve the situation.

Two story elements, however, are not yet worked out, and their incompleteness prepares the reader for more to come. First, the reader is made aware that the present moment is a pivotal one: not only has Emma's scheming met with reversal, but also the tables are turned in reference to the social-level suitability of two marriageable persons. Emma has been presuming that lowborn Harriet will do for Mr. Elton, but she is now surprised and provoked to note that toward *herself* he "should suppose himself her equal in connection or mind!—look down upon her friend, so well understanding the gradations of rank below him, and be so blind to what rose above, as to fancy himself shewing no presumption in addressing her!" Unless mere reversal is the main point being made—as it is not with Jane Austen, who is far more interested in the effects of emotion than in the momentary eruptions of emotion—more story obviously is to come. Second, in spite of Emma's new insight into events and herself and in spite of her new resolutions, the reader is warned that she is highly capable of relapse and that her lifelong habit of managing things has not come to full terms with itself, even on the level of self-deception. Furthermore, though nature gives respite for Emma and perhaps Mr. Elton to compose themselves, nature tends in no way to resolve the problems, which are human ones that still must be met by a very human Emma.

# CHAPTERS XVII–XVIII

*Summary*

With improved weather the John Knightleys leave for London, and on the same evening a note comes from Mr. Elton to Mr. Woodhouse, stating that at the entreaties of friends he is leaving in the morning for Bath and will not get to come by Hartfield before he goes. This is agreeably surprising news for Emma, for it leaves her relatively free to approach Harriet, to whom she goes the very next day. Her confession of events renews her first shame and brings tears from Harriet. In her simplicity and modesty Harriet will not complain, and her reaction impresses Emma, who is "really for the time convinced that Harriet was the superior creature of the two." Considering that her second duty is to promote Harriet's comfort, Emma gets her to Hartfield for needed kindness and amusement. Nonetheless, Harriet's continued belief that Mr. Elton is "all perfection" proves that she is "more resolutely in love than Emma had foreseen." Emma realizes that, until Harriet is cured, there can be "no true peace for herself."

Frank Churchill does not come in January after all, and Mrs. Weston is exceedingly disappointed. Emma is otherwise too involved to care much about Frank at the moment; but in putting on a false concern to cover her other feelings, she tells George about the further delay by Frank and says a good deal more than she feels. This leads to a disagreement with George, who thinks that Frank is avoiding his duty, and Emma is amused to perceive herself taking a side that is not in accord with her real opinion. Emma states that, in light of all the long conjectures about Frank and his coming, her idea of him is that "he can adapt his conversation to the taste of every body" and be universally agreeable. George's reply is that, if he turns out to be anything like that, "he will be the most insufferable fellow breathing!" Emma is quite surprised at the degree of his vexation, at what seems to be genuine anger. To dislike a young man only because he appears of a different disposition from himself is "unworthy the real liberality of mind which she was always used to acknowledge in him." Never before has she supposed he could be "unjust to the merit of another."

## Commentary

These two chapters represent the denouement following the climax of Volume One. This leveling-off action, obviously in a lower key than that of the two climactic chapters immediately preceding, for the moment tidies up the remaining threads of the dominant plot action of the first volume. Since Mr. Elton's part in this action is finished, he is removed from the locale. Emma makes her call upon Harriet and starts trying to mend the situation for her. The present possibility of a visit from Frank Churchill is terminated. Thus the first volume concludes a developing series of significant events through which inwardly the principal characters have been changed but which leaves their outward, material circumstances essentially unaltered, at least among themselves as a fixed social group. Each of the characters primarily involved—Emma, Harriet, Mr. Elton, George Knightley—is no closer to marrying one of the others than at the beginning of the volume. This outward non-change, then, focuses the spotlight of significance upon the inward change; and because of the limited point of view taken in the novel, the major portion of this change belongs to Emma, coming by way of revelation. Mr. Elton's revelation of his passion is important primarily because it leads Emma to a revelation about herself. Because of her self-deception she has deluded and misjudged others, and her shock of recognition—the long thoughts before going to bed and during the following days—is basically the (in this case unpleasant) discovery of the self.

In rounding out this volume, however, the author has prepared for much of what is to follow. There has been occasional mention of Jane Fairfax, of course, who is yet to be seen. But here in the denouement quite a bit of attention is directed toward Frank Churchill, who is also yet to come upon the scene. And to the perceptive reader the terminal and unusual reaction of George Knightley to Emma's interest in Frank, while it is presented with subtle artlessness and near offhandedness, will have its significance in both its final emphatic position and in the fact and object of his anger.

# VOLUME TWO

## CHAPTERS I-II

*Summary*

Emma and Harriet are walking one morning when they approach the house of Mrs. and Miss Bates. Though the latter is an inveterate and compulsive talker who in all kindness gives indiscriminate attention to the trivial and the important and who therefore is disliked by Emma, Emma decides that her calling upon them is overdue and that their talk will divert Harriet's thoughts from Mr. Elton. Talk of a letter from Mr. Elton is succeeded by Miss Bates's minute details of a letter from her niece Jane Fairfax, who after a two-year interval is to begin a three-month visit with the Bateses the very next week because the Campbells, with whom she lives, are leaving to visit their recently married daughter, Mrs. Dixon, in Ireland. From the details Emma conceives a lively, though unfounded, suspicion that Jane has aroused the affections of young Mr. Dixon, who not long ago saved her from falling off the boat into the water at Weymouth. However, still promising to read the letter, Miss Bates says that Jane's reason for coming is health: coming to Highbury will be good for the bad cold which she caught at Weymouth and which has lingered disagreeably ever since. Before the letter can be read, Emma and Harriet happily escape back to the street.

After being orphaned, Jane was taken into the family of Colonel Campbell, a friend of her military father. There she was "brought up for educating others" and became a close friend of the daughter her own age. In this elegant society her beauty and acquirements stand in contrast to those of the daughter, who has won Mr. Dixon. With the boring character of Miss Bates coloring her feelings, Emma does not like Jane and is sorry for her coming. But when Jane arrives, Emma is forced to admire her elegance to the point that she acquits her of having "seduced Mr. Dixon's affections" and even laments that Highbury affords "no young man worthy of giving her independence." When Jane visits Hartfield with her grandmother and aunt, however, Emma's feelings relapse, for Jane is

very reserved, wrapping her real opinions "in a cloak of politeness."
She is particularly reserved about Weymouth and the Dixons and
about Frank Churchill, who was at Weymouth at the same time. On
the latter all she will do is repeat the very general lip-service of
others, and Emma cannot forgive her.

## Commentary

The beginning of Volume Two not only introduces an entirely
new character, Jane Fairfax (prepared for earlier, of course), but
also indicates that Emma's flair for intrigue is far from being extin-
guished. Still trying to console Harriet for her "loss" of Mr. Elton,
she can nonetheless imagine an emotional entanglement for Jane
and also wish to manipulate her toward a suitable partner. Emma's
fluctuating tendency is exemplified in her initial dislike and jealousy
of Jane, her subsequent admiration for Jane's qualities and sorrow
for her penniless condition, and her final return to disliking the
orphan. Concomitant with, and perhaps causitive of, Emma's attitude is the fact that Jane is her first real competition in both acquirements and beauty.

A measure of Miss Austen's realism and satire is found in the
characterization of Miss Bates. Miss Bates is such a compulsive
talker that she jumps hurriedly from subject to subject, as if time
is too short for her necessity to vocalize everything that comes into
her life (she says practically nothing of herself except as being the
object of everyone's goodness), and treats everything as of equal
importance. The satire, however, lies not only in the delineation
of Miss Bates but also in the kind of society that will put up with
her; it is of course ambiguous satire, each element containing that
which is not admirable and that which is (Miss Bates, for instance,
is good intention personified).

## CHAPTERS III-IV

### Summary

Coming the next morning on business with Mr. Woodhouse,
George Knightley gives his approbation to Emma for being so

pleasant toward Jane, though the two disagree about the reason for
Jane's reserve. He is about to give Emma a piece of news when he
is interrupted by the arrival of Miss Bates and Miss Fairfax with
thanks for a hindquarter of pork sent them by the Woodhouses. Miss
Bates is also bursting with the news that Mr. Elton, who has been
away only four weeks, is going to be married to a Miss Hawkins
whom he has met at Bath. Jane still will not commit herself on anything, even on Mr. Elton, whom she has of course not yet met.
George leaves with the other two visitors, and Emma is left with her
father, who laments "that young people would be in such a hurry to
marry — and to marry strangers too," and with her concern about
how Harriet will feel when she learns the news.

After a heavy but short rain, Harriet arrives in a state of per-
turbation, but it is not because she has heard of Mr. Elton. Instead,
she has been detained by the rain at Ford's, the principal fashion-
able shop in Highbury, where she encountered Robert Martin and
his sister, who first ignored her and then came by to speak quite
amiably and kindly with her. Emma has to admit to herself that they
have acted worthily, but she is disturbed at Harriet's excitement
over meeting Robert again, and to assuage it she is obliged to hurry
on with the news about Mr. Elton. As Mr. Elton's rights to Harriet's
attention gradually revive, Emma is rather glad of the meeting at
Ford's for "deadening the first shock, without retaining any influence to alarm."

The Highbury rumors about Miss Hawkins are such good and
numerous ones that Mr. Elton needs to tell very little of her when
he returns. Her first name is Augusta and she possesses about ten
thousand pounds in fortune; since she and he have no one to please
except themselves, the wedding will be soon. Emma does not like
the pique and pretension that she now sees in Mr. Elton, and she
determines what she can of Miss Hawkins: that she is the younger
daughter of a Bristol merchant, that her parents are dead, and that
her older sister is married to a gentleman near Bristol. Emma does
not think very highly of these circumstances, but her thoughts and
hands are filled with Harriet, who sees and hears, or hears of, Mr.
Elton and his concerns at every turn before he leaves again
for Bath.

When a few days later Elizabeth Martin calls at Mrs. Goddard's and, finding Harriet not at home, leaves a note, Emma advises a return visit as best. It will be a social call to establish what Emma feels is the proper relationship among them, for she herself will take Harriet in the carriage, leave her at the farm, and return for her after only fifteen minutes. Her heart does not fully approve of the scheme, but she can think of nothing better.

## Commentary

These chapters continue the settling of the situation for Mr. Elton and Harriet, at the same time extending the subordinate plot thread of the Martins. Emma's sense of social distinction is further affirmed both in respect to the Martins and in her attitude toward what she learns of Augusta Hawkins. Jane is still something of an enigma, but one problem that Emma has set in motion becomes clear when she realizes that "Harriet was one of those, who, having once begun, would be always in love." She now sees her management of Harriet as a bit of a chore but also as a matter of course.

## CHAPTER V

### Summary

Harriet's visit to the Martins goes as Emma has hoped, for she picks up Harriet just as the acquaintance is about to become intimate again. On the way home they meet Mr. and Mrs. Weston, who have news that Frank Churchill will arrive the next day to stay an entire fortnight. Mr. Weston promises to bring him soon to Hartfield, and Mrs. Weston asks to be remembered at four the next afternoon when Frank is to arrive. The next morning Emma remembers at every opportunity and then is surprised when at noon she comes downstairs to find Mr. Weston and his son with her father. Frank appears to live up to his reputation, being good looking and lively and having "a well-bred ease of manner." Sure that he knows how to make himself agreeable, she wonders if he guesses that the Westons hope something will develop between her and him. He is all good breeding, even as his father leaves on business and he himself retires to visit the Bateses and Jane, the last with whom he has "the honour of being acquainted."

*Commentary*

In addition to introducing Frank Churchill, who is to be a major character in the novel in spite of his actual coming on the scene so late, the present chapter offers a contrast between the natural attraction of Harriet toward Robert Martin (whose presence on the short visit is felt more because he is not physically there) and the comparatively artificial attraction of Emma toward Frank — artificial because it is based, not upon any real association, but upon the unstated yet prescriptive hopes of the beloved Westons and upon the kind of predisposition that can be kindled by an expectant community in general. Both of these factors have worked successfully upon Emma's imagination, while it has been Robert as a reality that has worked upon Harriet.

As for Frank, to Emma at least he proves to be the all-pleasing young man she formerly pictured to George Knightley. It is worth remembering that, when she thus described him, she was still partly following an argumentative position opposite to her real opinion. One cannot be certain whether this was meant to be merely argumentative or laudatory; but in any event, having now met and talked with Frank, she is indeed "very well pleased with this beginning of the acquaintance." It is highly ironical that, as simpleminded Harriet's attention was directed toward Mr. Elton by Emma, strong-willed Emma's attention has been directed toward Frank at least to a great extent by others than herself.

## CHAPTERS VI-VII

*Summary*

The next morning Frank comes again with Mrs. Weston, and Emma decides to form her opinion of him by his behavior toward his stepmother. As the three of them tour Highbury by foot, he shows a liking for everything, and Emma is won over. As they pass the Crown Inn, where dances were once held, he seems rather bent on dancing. Recalling that he was to have visited the Bateses, Emma inquires and finds herself defending Jane Fairfax's complexion. After a visit to Ford's, she pursues the subject of Jane and learns that Mr. Dixon had preferred Jane's music to that of Miss Campbell, a statement that adds fuel to Emma's imagination. Quite gallantly Frank agrees with Emma about Jane's being reserved. When they pass the vicarage, Mr. Elton's house, Frank avers that the house would be big enough for any man living there with the woman he loved. All in all, Emma feels pleased with the new acquaintance.

The next day, however, her good opinion is shaken when Frank goes all the way to London for only a haircut. She can overlook such an act, though, for he may be forming an attachment for her. Others too see it only as a youthful whim, but not George Knightley, who thinks Frank "just the trifling, silly fellow I took him for."

The *nouveau riche* Coles are planning a dinner party, and though Emma some time past decided never to accept an invitation of theirs, she is irked that she and her father have not been invited now, since all their closest friends have been. While the Westons are visiting at Hartfield, that very invitation comes with a just explanation for its delay. Since she really wants to attend, Emma lets herself be persuaded, though her father declines so much activity. Mr. Woodhouse is finally coaxed into allowing Emma to stay late at the party, and everything is thus settled.

## Commentary

Emma is letting herself be "taken in" by Frank in spite of the fact that she sees he is determined to please everyone. She enjoys toying with the possibility that he is growing fond of her, and she lets this enjoyment blind her first into overlooking some negative manifestations of his character and second into confiding in him too quickly with some of her attitude toward Jane. Only later will the reader know it, but, somewhat like Harriet, Emma is having her feelings misled. One thing about Emma, though, remains constant: her approval of a static social hierarchy (Harriet's unknown situation being a notable exception), indicated in her attitude toward the Coles. When this belief comes in conflict with her natural bent for social entertainment, however, she lets herself be persuaded because others have accepted the Coles, because the invitation is in good taste and properly solicits her as an "honor," and because she can attend out of a partial sense of *noblesse oblige*. The satire in her "letting herself be persuaded" should be obvious.

### CHAPTER VIII

*Summary*

Frank returns from London and evidences no discomposure about the purpose of the trip; but Emma is ready not only to overlook that but also to wonder how soon, in light of his possible feeling for her, she should "throw coldness into her air" toward him.

When she reaches the Coles' for the party, she praises George Knightley—who for once has brought out his carriage—for being a proper gentleman for the occasion; he only laughs good-humoredly. As those who are to come early for dinner arrive, Frank seats himself agreeably beside her. During the meal Mrs. Cole reports the news that a new, large pianoforte arrived that day for Jane, who has been puzzled about it, though of course it must be from Colonel Campbell. Emma thinks that Mr. Dixon has sent it surreptitiously, and Frank agrees in such a polite way with her words that he seems to be agreeing about Mr. Dixon, who had preferred Jane's playing to Miss Campbell's. Ambiguously he concludes his remarks about the instrument by saying, "And now I can see it in no other light than as an offering of love."

The ladies are in the drawing room after dinner when the other ladies—including Miss Bates and Jane—arrive for the remainder of the party. As soon as the men join them, Frank makes his way directly to Emma. After an interruption by Mr. Cole, Emma sees Frank looking intently across the room at Jane, but he says that it is only on account of the way her hair is done and goes over purportedly to ask her about it. Mrs. Weston joins Emma to say that George's carriage has brought Jane and Miss Bates and that she thinks a match is making "between Mr. Knightley and Jane Fairfax." Emma will not believe this, declaring that "Mr. Knightley must not marry!" and thereby cut little Henry off from inheriting the Donwell Abbey estates. She even mimics Miss Bates to indicate the absurdity of George's ever marrying Jane, but Mrs. Weston hints that the pianoforte may have come from George.

Emma is asked to play and is joined in singing by Frank. Then while Jane plays and Frank joins her also in singing, George talks with Emma in such a way that she is convinced that he would never send a gift secretly to anybody. When the first of two dances is proposed, Frank secures Emma's hand for it and George, instead of asking Jane or anybody else to dance, goes and talks with Mr. Cole. Emma feels "no longer an alarm for Henry" and lets herself enjoy the dancing.

## Commentary

Emma continues to let herself be impressed by Frank, while he adroitly replies to her suspicions about Jane with words that seem to agree with her and sometimes do. The reader may be beginning to wonder some about his words and actions, but Emma is not. She is, in fact, so optimistically sure of things and of herself that unconsciously she puts George in the same category of "not marrying" with herself. She does this in a context which involves another instance of reversal, though a milder one than the climactic one in the first volume: Mrs. Weston is now the matchmaker. For a moment, at least, her and Emma's roles are reversed; and through this Miss Austen may be making a wry comment on the influences of human relationships.

The reader who finishes the novel and then re-reads this chapter will find, as he often will in other chapters, a great deal of irony —for instance, in the manner in which Emma (and perhaps the reader also on a first perusal) is shrewdly misled by Frank's conversation and observations, likewise in Emma's reason given as to why George must never marry. But there is also immediate irony which the reader can find, for example, in George's reply to Emma's congratulating him for bringing his carriage to the party. Though irony always contains some kind of special truth, in this case it is both obvious and realistic.

*Summary*

The day after the party Emma is still delighted but so chagrined at Jane's musical ability that she sits and practices "vigorously an hour and a half" before Harriet comes in. The latter's references to the Martins make Emma feel obliged to accompany her, as protection, to Ford's shop. Standing in the doorway at Ford's, Emma sees Mrs. Weston and Frank approaching the Bates house. Seeing her, they come forward and Frank lets the two women convince him that he should accompany Mrs. Weston to see Jane's pianoforte. Harriet has just waveringly managed to complete her transactions when Mrs. Weston and Miss Bates arrive and invite them over to appraise the new instrument. Back at home Miss Bates is surprised that Frank has not completed fastening the rivet of Mrs. Bates's spectacles, but he says that he has been helping Jane make the instrument steady while Mrs. Bates was asleep by the fire.

When Jane plays, Frank harps upon the Campbells and Ireland to Emma, with innuendos about the instrument. He seems to want Jane to hear him. When Miss Fairfax smiles at some of his words, Emma, who has been feeling sorry for her, now decides that she is "cherishing very reprehensible feelings."

George Knightley comes by on horseback, and Miss Bates talks with him from the casement of an adjoining room so loudly that all can hear. He offers to bring something for her from Kingston, but she wants nothing — except to rattle on with her talk and to get him inside if possible. When she thanks him effusively for some apples he recently sent them, he is embarrassed and says he must hurry on. Shortly afterward the other guests leave also.

*Commentary*

Miss Austen sums up the kind of character that Emma is when, as Emma looks over the nearly blank streets of Highbury, the author says: "A mind lively and at ease, can do with seeing nothing, and can see nothing that does not answer." Frank too has apparently seen this in Emma, for he continues to encourage her suspicions about Jane and Mr. Dixon. Later the reader, who may already have some suspicions of his own about Frank, will learn that Frank is using this conjecture, along with his attentions to Emma, to disguise his real situation. He does a very good job of covering up, and it is this aspect of the novel that has led some critics to point out that on one limited level it is a mystery story. Miss Bates is closer to something like a discovery than she knows when she is incredulous about Frank's not having finished the simple repairs to Mrs. Bates's spectacles. Mrs. Bates's being asleep by the fire has left Frank and Jane alone together.

Humor and attendant satire become paramount when George arrives on horseback and talks with Miss Bates, who is far from being unhappy at having to shout her words to him from the house. His generous nature is obvious throughout the scene; also is his abrupt common sense, which is in comic conflict with Miss Bates's urge to talk at length, for he politely and successfully cuts her short. His continuing attitude toward Frank is illustrated when, about to say that he will come inside for five minutes, he learns that Frank and Mrs. Weston are inside and quickly says that he does not have enough time and that Miss Bates's room is already full enough. Crowning the comic scene is Miss Bates's insistence upon relaying the conversation to the drawing room, where the amused group has obviously already heard every word.

## CHAPTERS XI-XII

### Summary

One evening at Randalls, Frank and Emma become determined to set up an evening for a real dance. Mr. Woodhouse is naturally against such a scheme for reasons of health, but the Westons are quite for it as they measure rooms to decide their suitability and the number of couples wanted. Late the next morning Frank arrives at Hartfield to announce that the dance will be held at the Crown Inn. When Mr. Woodhouse argues against the place, Frank adroitly answers his objections and takes Emma off to the Crown, which the Westons are inspecting. "They can do nothing satisfactorily without you," he tells Emma. After they have really settled the questions about using the place, Frank suggests that they need "a large council," which should include Miss Bates. This leads to his going for both the aunt and the niece. Since Frank has written the Churchills for permission to extend his visit a few days, everything for the dance seems to be in order, especially for the Westons, who note that Frank has "secured" Emma for the first two dances.

Word comes that Frank may stay longer, and Emma is now certain of her ball except for "Mr. Knightley's provoking indifference about it," an indifference much in contrast to Jane's animated hopes for the social event.

Two days later everything is overthrown when a letter comes stating that Mrs. Churchill is ill and that Frank must return home immediately. Frank comes by Hartfield to say goodbye and Emma learns that he has already done the same at the Bates household. He seems about to declare himself on something when he pauses in mid-sentence as if to read her thoughts. Afraid of what he might be about to say, Emma calmly continues about the rightness of his visit to the Bateses. There is silence, during which he sighs. Once again he breaks off in the middle of a sentence, and Emma thinks that he is more in love with her than she supposed. But at that moment Mr. Weston enters and Frank, saying that he will look forward to hearing from them in Highbury, leaves with his father.

For Emma it is a sad change, with no more meetings with Frank and now with no immediate probability of a ball. Quite rationally she begins to think "that she *must* be a little in love with him, in spite of every previous determination against it." George, who she thinks will be glad there is to be no ball, on the contrary shows "no truimphant happiness"; however, Jane Fairfax's composure about the situation is "odious," in spite of her being unwell and suffering from headaches.

*Commentary*

Emma is deceiving herself more and more about Frank. He is a charming companion, but in addition she chooses to interpret his

words and actions in only one way: as they might apply to herself.
This is part of the ironic reversal in which her attitude, for a change,
is being conditioned by others, not the least of whom is Frank himself. The reversal is possible, though, because of the continuity of
Emma's vanity. In the moments before parting, she assumes that
he is about to declare something in reference to her. Later the reader
learns that he was about to say something quite different, that he
would have been giving her credit for insight that she did not have.
The irony is delayed but nonetheless is there for the reader who
looks back at the politely clever ways in which Frank manages to
come in contact with Jane or finds excuses for bringing her upon
a scene.

Among the instances of satire here, the reader might notice the
continued presentation of Mr. Woodhouse's character, the undue
concern about getting the opinions of others in reference to using
the Crown Inn for the ball, and the way in which the wish becomes
father to acceptance as the group inspects the faults of the Crown.
At the end of this section is brief but effective contrast between
Frank and George and between Emma and Jane.

## CHAPTERS XIII-XIV

### Summary

Emma continues "to entertain no doubt of her being in love"
with Frank, but "the conclusion of every imaginary declaration on
his side was that she *refused him*." Though she is certain that he
is in love, she begins to suspect that he is not really necessary to her
happiness. When she reads a letter that Mrs. Weston receives from
Frank, she still finds that she can "do without the writer"; but struck
by a reference in the letter to her "beautiful little friend" Harriet,
she begins to think of scheming.

Now that Frank is gone, the center of attention becomes the
expected arrival of the Eltons. Harriet is in such a flutter about this
that Emma, to divert her friend for her good, reproaches her for
not thinking of Emma and the pain that the constant reference to the
Eltons causes her. Harriet reacts with such concern that Emma

later muses on her tenderness of heart and wifely possibilities, concluding thus: "I mention no names; but happy the man who changes Emma for Harriet!"

Mrs. Elton is first seen at church, but not long afterward Emma, taking Harriet to get the confrontation over with, pays the newlyweds a short visit. Emma feels that she sees in Augusta Elton not much elegance but too much ease for a young woman who is both a bride and a stranger. When the visit is returned, she becomes convinced that Augusta is "a vain woman," for she talks too much about her "brother Mr. Suckling's seat" of Maple Grove and about his barouche-landau, which they use for "exploring." She is overly familiar with her recommendation of the "advantages of Bath" for Mr. Woodhouse; then after denying any real ability with music, she insists that she and Emma, as town leaders, must form a musical society. Revealing that they have been calling at Randalls, she offers hasty, brief praise of the Westons and refers to another visitor there as Knightley, whom she has then met for the first time.

After the Eltons are gone, Emma inwardly expresses her outrage at this "insufferable woman" who, having never seen George before, glibly calls him Knightley. The woman is worse than she has imagined. When Mr. Woodhouse states that he should have paid his respects to Augusta because "Not to wait upon a bride is very remiss," Emma chides him as no friend to matrimony and states that what he says he should have done is "encouragement to marry." He wants to argue the point, but Emma drops it, her mind returning "to Mrs. Elton's offences, and long, very long, did they occupy her."

*Commentary*

Something close to reversal begins to occur in these two chapters. Emma obviously has not ended her propensity to manage others and can even shift her own feelings for Frank into another possible "management" for Harriet. Marriage, of course, is still the focal point for her scheming. Now a new character, Augusta Elton, is introduced as one who also likes to manage things. In a sense Augusta combines the worst characteristics of both Emma and Miss

Bates. Like Miss Bates, she is an inveterate and domineering talker; but unlike the spinster, she seems lacking in genuine goodwill and in any compensating self-effacement. Like Emma, she has an over-riding urge to manage; but unlike her new acquaintance, she obviously is wanting in good breeding and taste and apparently is ready to pass judgment on and manage any and everything that comes into view. We are never told directly that Emma sees something of herself in Augusta; but the rector's new wife will be another major factor in Emma's gradual maturing into self-knowledge, for Augusta is a flagrant example of how far one can go in self-importance and in "management." At the moment, concentrating upon the vulgar reference to George as Knightley, Emma can analyze the newcomer only to the point of calling her an insufferable woman because she is crude and brash.

At this point in the story Emma is beginning to get over another crisis: her feeling that she is in love with Frank Churchill. The practical and reasoning side of her nature is starting to reassert itself. Interestingly enough Augusta, in addition to being a revelatory foil for Emma, serves her in another psychological way. Since something or someone is needed to replace the diminishing personal significance of Frank, Augusta will allow her vent for both emotion and reaction. The "insufferable woman" helps her get over the involvement — such as it is — with Frank.

## CHAPTER XV

*Summary*

Emma finds nothing to change her ill opinion of Augusta; in fact, while Mr. Elton appears happy and even proud of his wife, she alters her feelings toward Emma and becomes quite unpleasant toward Harriet. She takes a great fancy to Jane Fairfax and declares she will "help" her. What surprises Emma is that Jane tolerates and accepts the woman's attentions.

When Jane gets another invitation to join the Campbells in Ireland and declines, Emma feels that she "must have some motive, more powerful than appears, for refusing." Mrs. Weston and George suggest that Jane lets the Eltons entertain her because she must at times get away from the Bates household. This is Emma's opportunity to press George about how highly he regards Jane; but brought to the point, he assures her that he will never ask Jane to marry him, saying that she has the fault of lacking an open temper in spite of her other virtues. Emma feels that she has won her argument on this with Mrs. Weston, but the latter is not so certain.

## Commentary

Though Emma is not consciously aware of it, she is getting a rather good dose of comeuppance from the "managing" Mrs. Elton, and more is to come. Otherwise, so far as Emma is concerned, two elements of plot movement develop here: George's supposed interest in Jane is clarified, while the puzzle of Jane itself continues and is augmented by Jane's toleration of Mrs. Elton.

## Summary                                    CHAPTER XVI

Everybody seems to be inviting the Eltons for dinners and evening parties. Emma too feels that she must satisfy the situation by giving them a dinner, to which she also invites the Westons, George, and Harriet. To her happiness Harriet begs off, and Jane is invited in her place. Emma is apprehensive when she learns that John Knightley is to come on that very day to leave his two oldest boys for a visit, for Mr. Woodhouse does not believe in more than eight at the dinner table and John is likely to be disagreeable. Things turn out well, though, when Mr. Weston has to go out of town on unexpected business that day and when John proves agreeable after all. In fact, John is quite affable with Jane, whom he has seen that day on her way to the post office. When he talks about how marriage and a family change one's eagerness about getting letters, her reaction is "a blush, a quivering lip, a tear in the eye."

Talk of Jane's walk to the post office in the rain reaches Mrs. Elton, who "will not allow her to do such a thing again." She is extremely officious about it, declaring that her servant will pick up the Bateses' mail too, although Jane insists otherwise and changes the subject. Talk of handwriting leads George to say that "Emma's hand" is stronger than the style of her sister and to add a bit later that Frank's writing "is too small — wants strength." As the group starts for the dinner table, Emma wonders about Jane's constant morning walks for the mail and suspects that she does it "in full expectation of hearing from some one very dear." She determines not to utter a word to hurt Jane's feelings.

*Commentary*

In addition to illustrating further Mr. Woodhouse's fussiness and Emma's sense of social obligation, this chapter deepens the mystery of Jane. Though Emma still thinks that the problem is Mr. Dixon, she nonetheless seems to be developing a degree of sympathy for, if not understanding of, Jane. Excepting perhaps the reader, no one seems really to notice the compliment that George utters about "Emma's hand."

## CHAPTERS XVII-XVIII

*Summary*

When the ladies return to the drawing room after dinner, they make two distinct parties, for Augusta slights Emma and takes Jane aside to discuss finding a situation as governess for her. Jane insists that she does not want to look for a position yet, but Augusta is determined to be of help and rattles on until the men join the ladies. At that moment Mr. Weston, returned from his business trip, joins the party, to the astonishment of John, who cannot understand a man who, after a long day of business, will leave his warm home to come out on a cold, sleety April evening just for socializing. Mr. Weston was expected, of course, but he also has news of Frank, whose letter to Mrs. Weston the husband has opened. That Frank will soon be coming again pleases Mrs. Weston, displeases George and Mr. Woodhouse, and makes Emma weigh her feelings and "the degree of her agitation, which she rather thought was considerable."

Moving on to give the news to Augusta, who has not yet met Frank, Mr. Weston states the details. Because of Mrs. Churchill's illness, about which he has his doubts, all the Churchills will be coming for a stay in London the very next month and Frank will be able to make the sixteen-mile trip to Highbury quite often. John, who must leave for home early the next morning, turns to Emma to say that she must not spoil his two boys and must send them home if they prove troublesome. When she says that cannot possibly happen, he knowingly mentions her being so "much more engaged with company than you used to be.... The difference which Randalls, Randalls alone makes in your goings-on, is very great." George cries that the boys can be sent to Donwell, that he has leisure. In reply Emma offers a spirited self-defense against the charge of frequent new social engagements and insists that she is at home much more than George. This is apparently the reaction that George wants, for "Mr. Knightley seemed to be trying not to smile; and succeeded without difficulty, upon Mrs. Elton's beginning to talk to him."

## Commentary

Volume Two now ends, but without an external climax as in Volume One. There is, however, a definite rising, climaxing, and sloughing plot action in Emma's feelings for Frank Churchill, but this is internal and it is not yet entirely resolved. Some mystery has been hinted in regard to Jane and to Frank, but it is not really yet developed—much less resolved—and it serves primarily to underscore the further probability of Emma's self-deception. Augusta is introduced as a new conflictive element for Emma, one from which she *may* subconsciously learn something of herself; in fact, the brash and willful Augusta is one of Miss Austen's most subtle plot elements, for the author never has Emma directly confront herself with the Augusta in herself—Augusta is a negative force helping almost unperceived toward a positive end.

More specifically, in these concluding chapters Augusta is the butt of immediate satire. She is blithely unaware that she strikes herself when she says that "modern ease often disgusts me," and she creates a reader's delight when, in talking with Mr. Weston about her sister, she realizes that she has caught herself in her own cross fire of coy modesty and proud pretensions.

Since John's two sons enter these final chapters of Volume Two, it is perhaps worth noting that children and servants are merely in the background throughout the novel. The reader is never made to see them or feel their presence, though when the reader looks very closely, servants in particular are in abundance. One reason is that in this society servants (even one for the poor Bateses) and perhaps children are taken for granted. Another is that the satire of the novel is based, not upon general realism, but upon social realism as found in a provincial community where servants and children do not figure socially. Servants and children will conform to their predictable natures, but only the adult socialites have the freedom and wherewithal to create or inherit a code of manners and to let their conformities and aberrations be measured by that code.

Once again in rounding out a volume, Miss Austen points toward Frank Churchill and his imminent presence in Highbury. Also once again her concluding scene involves a kind of cross-purpose relationship between Emma and George.

# VOLUME THREE

## CHAPTERS I-II

### Summary

Two months have passed since Frank Churchill left Highbury, and Emma is convinced that her own attachment has "really subsided into a mere nothing." Yet she cannot help anticipating something decisive when he comes again. Soon after the Churchills remove to London, he rides down for a couple of hours, coming immediately to Hartfield, where it appears clear to Emma that, though he is fluttered and restless, he is "less in love than he had been." The quarter-hour visit is the only one for ten days. Then the Churchills, for Mrs. Churchill's health, move again to Richmond, where they will stay for two months, only nine miles from Highbury. Such closeness makes the ball at the Crown Inn a certainty.

The day for it arrives, and Emma goes early to give her requested opinion of the place to the Westons. Shortly one and then another carriage arrive with cousins whose opinions are also wanted. Frank stands beside Emma but seems anxious for things to get started. The Eltons arrive and send their carriage on for Miss Bates and Jane. Augusta's talking with Frank leads her vocally to decide that she likes him just as he and Mr. Weston go to escort in Miss Fairfax and Miss Bates, the latter already erupting with incessant chatter. Upon being questioned, Frank whispers to Emma that he does not like Augusta.

Emma does not like to but has to let Augusta begin the ball, but she is more disturbed by George Knightley's not dancing at all. Instead, he seems to be observing her as the ball proceeds pleasantly until, as the last two dances before supper begin, Harriet has no partner. At first sauntering about, Mr. Elton stops before some of the older ladies and offers to dance with two of them, then obviously and thoroughly slights Harriet. All of this is seen with approval by Augusta and with hot distaste by Emma, who a moment later is delighted to see George leading Harriet to the set and to see that his dancing is as extremely good as she has guessed. After supper Emma gets a chance to thank him. Both wondering and guessing why the Eltons feel themselves her enemies, he criticizes them and commends Harriet for her good qualities. With the dancing about to resume, he asks her with whom she is to dance. Hesitating, she replies, "With you, if you will ask me." He does.

### Commentary

Plotting is well developed in these two chapters. Emma is no longer worried about herself and Frank, but she is curious about his present restless behavior yet fails to observe the little attentions that he pays to Jane. The Eltons show their true colors, and it is to Frank's credit that he does not like Augusta. But George is the hero of the hour in reacting so gallantly after Mr. Elton's obvious rudeness to Harriet. Slowly and quietly Miss Austen is showing him to be by far the most admirable man in Highbury, just as Emma, in spite of her willful imagination, is the most interesting and admirable woman there. The reader, aware of Emma's past attitudes and inclinations, should be able to detect the modulated beginning of story conflict when, at the very end of Chapter II, George emphatically agrees with Emma that they are indeed not brother and sister.

The satire of caricature is continued here with Augusta and Miss Bates. But the broader and more subtle satire of a community and its fluttery emphasis on giving a ball is localized in the comic scene in which, after Emma has come early to give her asked opinion, others arrive for the same reason. The scene is one that also has its share in Emma's slowly maturing into self-knowledge: in reference to Mr. Weston she now feels "that to be the favourite and intimate of a man who had so many intimates and confidantes, was not the very first distinction in the scale of vanity." This is conscious realization. An unconscious sort, treated without satire, comes in the concluding scene with George, for at the moment Emma relates her happy feelings toward George only to his rescue of Harriet and to his agreeing with her about Harriet and the Eltons.

## CHAPTER III

### Summary

The next morning Emma feels that Mr. Elton's slight of the night before will cure Harriet of her infatuation. Emma also does not regret that she will not see Frank, who has to be back at Richmond by the middle of the day. She is therefore surprised when Frank appears with a fainting Harriet on his arm. After Harriet has actually fainted, Emma learns that on a morning walk along the Richmond road her pretty friend has met with and been bullied by a party of gypsies, from whom Frank has luckily rescued her. When Harriet recovers, Frank must go on his belated way and Emma ponders upon how seemingly "every thing united to promise the most interesting consequences" for Harriet and Frank. But she contents herself that she will "not stir a step, nor drop a hint" to further her wish: it will be "a mere passive scheme." Meanwhile a warning about the gypsies is spread over Highbury, though the gypsies have hurried off before the town's young ladies can even begin to panic.

## Commentary

The important action of this chapter is not that which occurs completely "offstage" with the gypsies, but that which presents Emma's still-developing character. She is as much a schemer as ever, but her scheming is now modified. Trying to tell herself that she has practiced "enough of interference," she hopes to stick to passive wishing. Her imagination is as strong as ever, but she is at least trying to cope with her willfulness.

## CHAPTER IV

### Summary

A few days later Harriet appears with a small parcel in her hand, declaring that she can now see nothing extraordinary in Mr. Elton and showing Emma that the parcel is marked with "Most precious treasures" on the top. Taking from it a piece of court plaster and the end of an old pencil which had belonged to Mr. Elton and which she has carefully saved, she throws them behind the fire for Emma to see. Not many days afterward Harriet says that she will never marry and then continues inaudibly but with the final words: "so superior to Mr. Elton!" From their talking in very general and vague terms, Emma concludes that her friend is in love with Frank and both cautions and encourages her, thinking that, though he is her superior, such an attachment is "no bad thing for her friend."

### Commentary

The action of this chapter speaks for itself, but one should note the curious mixture of pathos and bathos in the character of Harriet and note also the conflictive elements in Emma, who in one breath feels shame for her part in the Elton affair and in the next breath encourages her friend along the same line. Worthy of notice also is the verbal irony in the polite and misleading generalizations that wrongly confirm Emma's guess as to who Harriet's new object of attachment is.

## CHAPTER V

### Summary

During the month of June it is learned that Jane will stay two more months with the Bateses, and George grows to dislike Frank even more. In fact, Frank is on many minds: "While so many were devoting him to Emma, and Emma herself making him over to Harriet, Mr. Knightley began to suspect him of some inclination to trifle with Jane Fairfax." George has seen certain looks pass between Frank and Jane, and one evening during a group meeting at Hartfield Frank mentions news of Mr. Perry which Mrs. Weston says she did not write him because she did not know it until this very moment. Frank says he must have dreamed it, but it turns out that Miss Bates has known it as a secret. The "dream," however, is dropped as the group goes indoors and begins a word game, which George carefully observes. He notes that Frank puts before Jane a puzzle that leads to the word *blunder* and that another which spells *Dixon* so displeases her that she turns to Miss Bates for them to go. George remains behind with the idea of "trying to preserve" Emma, but Emma states emphatically that there is nothing between Frank and Jane, that "I can *answer* for its being so on his" side. "She spoke with a confidence which staggered, with a satisfaction which silenced, Mr. Knightley," who soon afterward takes a hasty leave.

### Commentary

Both the mystery of Frank and Jane and the observant sensibility of George are intensified in this chapter. The chapter is devoted almost entirely to plot action, but a parallel ironic development is worth noting: just as the verbal irony of generalization in the preceding chapter has misled Emma, here her emphatic generalization about Frank misleads George. In both instances it is Emma's wording that causes misunderstanding, the damaging vagueness resulting from the conflict between the urge to communicate and the need for polite restraint.

*Summary*

Mrs. Weston is expecting a baby, and Emma and Mr. Weston plan a quiet "exploring" trip to Box Hill. Augusta has of course been long wanting to make such a trip, and Mr. Weston suggests that his party and that of the Eltons unite, an idea that Emma does not like but accepts. When a lame carriage horse throws everything into "sad uncertainty," George answers Augusta that she should come to Donwell for strawberries instead. This immediately becomes a party, for which she insists that she do all the inviting of guests. But George is firm, saying that the only married woman he will ever "allow to invite what guests she pleases to Donwell" is Mrs. Knightley—"and, till she is in being, I will manage such matters myself." Augusta tries to pass this off humorously, finally only making an ass of herself. Later the lame horse mends and the trip to Box Hill is settled for the day after the party at Donwell.

Emma has not been to Donwell for some time, and on the day of the party she looks over the place with "honest pride and complacency" since it is a "family" estate now because of the nephews who will inherit it. Except for Frank, everyone is there as they gather strawberries and find seats in the shade. Augusta badgers Jane about accepting "a most desirable situation" until Jane suggests a walk to see the gardens. During this activity Emma sees George and Harriet strolling and talking by themselves, and she joins them before they all go indoors to eat. Frank still has not arrived when all but Emma, who stays behind with Mr. Woodhouse, go to see the old Abbey fish ponds. Emma is alone in the hallway when Jane appears "with a look of escape," saying that she is going to walk home. She will not accept the offer of a carriage, giving as reason that she is "wearied in spirits" and needs the walk. Shortly after she goes, Frank arrives "out of humour," observing that he has met Jane on the way and that he will not eat because it is so hot. Even as she gets him to eat something, Emma is glad to be through being in love with him. He tells her that he needs a change, that he is sick of England and wants to go abroad; but when the rest of the party return, his party-going inclination leads him to say that if *Emma* wants him to stay and join the group to Box Hill the next day, he will. "She smiled her acceptance...."

## Commentary

As this chapter well indicates, George is becoming more important in the plot. After his conversation with Augusta, it should be clear to the reader (if it has not already been) that he too is interested in marriage. He has earlier stated that he values good sense, strength, and openness in a wife; he now makes plain the kind of honor and consideration he will give her. At the same time he rather quietly but surely demonstrates his ability to deal with a wife who is overbearing and silly. When Augusta wishes she had a donkey to ride dust-free to the party, he says that Donwell Lane is never dusty but adds, "Come on a donkey, however, if you prefer it.... I would wish every thing to be as much to your taste as possible."

A notable contrast is seen between Emma and Augusta during the party at Donwell. Augusta is still the officious and obnoxious manager, forcing her "help" upon poor Jane. On the other hand, almost as if Donwell has a sobering and symbolic effect on her, Emma not once tries any of her usual scheming. Once, when Frank is mentioned, she looks at Harriet only to observe that she behaves very well and betrays no emotion; and that is as close as she comes to willfulness, except for one later mere observation. Otherwise she seems to be quite at peace with herself and ready to offer understanding and pity to Jane. Obviously, if she wished, for Harriet's sake she could urge Frank to accompany them to Box Hill, but she does not do so. The decision to go is strictly Frank's.

The mystery of Jane and Frank is developed only briefly, just a bit to cloud the issue. Janes leaves the party early, but we do not know what has wearied her spirits. When Frank finally arrives, he looks "very deplorable." But being delayed by Mrs. Churchill's illness has never appeared to bother him before, and his being out of humor with the weather is hardly rational. In each case we know only that the man is upset about something.

## CHAPTER VII

*Summary*

The day for "exploring" at Box Hill is a fine one as the ladies go there by carriage and the men on horseback. But there is a lack of union among them once there, and they break into little parties, Emma with Frank and Harriet. Frank is not only dull but also silent and stupid until the entire group sits down. Then he is extremely gallant toward Emma, and the two talk quite flirtatiously while the others say little or nothing. Frank makes a game of things by saying that Emma is presiding (an idea that makes Augusta swell) and that each person is to say something entertaining: either one very clever thing "or two things moderately clever—or three things very dull indeed." When Miss Bates exclaims that she will automatically do the last thing, Emma cannot resist saying, "Ah! ma'am, but there may be a difficulty. Pardon me—but you will be limited as to number —only three at once." It takes Miss Bates a moment to catch her meaning and then blush at the pain it causes. Mr. Weston leads off with a conundrum that is a flattering compliment of Emma, after which Augusta immediately excuses herself and her husband to go off walking.

Frank comments ironically on the "Happy couple!" and makes remarks about men and women meeting in the unnatural surroundings of resorts and the ill luck that it can generate. When Jane demurs, he bows in submission and then tells Emma in a lively tone to find a wife for him: "I am in no hurry. Adopt her, educate her." Emma agrees in the same tone and thinks of Harriet, as Jane takes her aunt to join the Eltons and George soon follows.

When it is time to go, George joins Emma beside her carriage and reproaches her for being "so unfeeling to Miss Bates." She is sorry but tries to laugh it off. However, George is serious and reasons at length that, because Miss Bates is poor, she deserves compassion and forbearance. He concludes thus: "I will tell you truths while I can, satisfied with proving myself your friend by very faithful counsel, and trusting that you will some time or other do me greater justice than you can do now." He leaves while she is silent with anger at herself and then reproaches herself for not having taken leave of him. The more she thinks of it, the more she is mortified and grieved: "How could she have been so brutal, so cruel to Miss Bates!" With only a silent Harriet in the carriage with her, "Emma felt the tears running down her cheeks almost all the way home."

## Commentary

To realize how much of a crisis this chapter is, the reader must come back to it after finishing the book. He will then see how Frank's flirtation with Emma has double meaning, that it very much involves Jane, for under the surface is a lovers' quarrel. It is for this reason that in the beginning Frank is silent and dull, and it is also for this reason that, as the Eltons walk away, he takes the opportunity to speak disparagingly of people's meeting at resorts. The reader who comes back to the chapter will be able to view Jane's situation with sympathetic understanding, and he will be able to see Frank's actions and comments as cruel but also psychologically believable as those of a lover.

Emma's crisis involves three things. First, she is over her attachment to Frank to the point of merely flirting. Second, she gets an actual though jesting invitation from Frank to find him a wife who, except for the hazel eyes (really hers) which he mentions, sounds very much like Harriet (since he is a perceptive young man, one wonders if he has guessed Emma's scheming and deliberately puts in one confusing detail); in terms of plot this is a test of Emma's determination to be strictly passive about the scheme. Third, after many years of containment Emma publicly expresses one part of her true feeling for Miss Bates and, in thereby bringing upon herself the reproaches of George, begins to realize how much his opinion of her matters. Her tears represent her own good nature, her sense of Miss Bates's goodness, and her sense of George's concern. Her own basic balance of good sense is also represented when she answers George about Miss Bates: "I know there is not a better creature in the world: but you must allow, that what is good and what is ridiculous are most unfortunately blended in her." Except perhaps for George, this last clause could be Miss Austen's ironic summation of practically every "creature" in the novel.

# CHAPTER VIII

## Summary

As Emma spends the whole evening at backgammon with her father, she still feels wretched. Earlier than usual, she pays a visit to the Bateses the next morning, determined to make amends if possible. Wishing very much to give pleasure, she enters the house as Miss Bates and Jane seem to be escaping into the adjoining room. When Miss Bates returns, things are momentarily strained until Emma asks about Jane and Miss Bates becomes her old self, recounting in detail that Jane has accepted a situation as governess, that Mrs. Elton brought it about, and that Jane is to leave within a fortnight. It all came about the evening before at Mrs. Elton's: right before tea had come word that Frank had left for Richmond; shortly after tea Jane had agreed to accept the situation which Augusta had found. Emma is struck by the difference of importance between Mrs. Churchill and Jane Fairfax. She sits "musing on the difference of woman's destiny" as Miss Bates talks of the disposition of the pianoforte until Emma takes her leave.

## Commentary

Emma's success in mollifying Miss Bates demonstrates the goodwill and basic kind intentions of both women. As the reader will see, Jane's decision to take a job is vital to the working out of one major part of the plot; but it also works in the direction of Emma's growth in knowledge as she muses on woman's destiny.

# CHAPTER IX

## Summary

Emma is still pensive when she reaches home to find that George and Harriet have arrived during her absence. George is about to go to London for a few days, and his grave manner assures Emma that he has not forgiven her. When Mr. Woodhouse asks about the Bateses, Jane colors, though she notes in George "an instantaneous impression in her favour." With a glow of regard, he presses her hand and is about to kiss it but lets it go. She is nonetheless greatly satisfied that he had the thought of doing it, and they part thorough friends, though she is very sorry not to have come back earlier for the pleasure of talking with him.

The following day news comes that Mrs. Churchill has died, a fact that tends to raise her in the estimation of Highbury. Emma now feels that an attachment between Frank and Harriet has "nothing to encounter." She notes that Harriet behaves with "great self-command" upon hearing the news.

Emma wishes very much "to show attention to Jane Fairfax, whose prospects were closing, while Harriet's opened." An invitation to visit Hartfield, however, is refused; and Mr. Perry reports that Jane has severe headaches and nervous fever. An offer of Emma's carriage at any hour is also refused. Determined to be of help, Emma takes the carriage over, but she gets to talk with only Miss Bates. Jane will not see her. Learning that Jane will eat nothing, Emma sends some superior arrowroot, which is returned. When Emma afterward learns that on that very afternoon Jane was seen wandering about the meadows, she is very sorry to realize "that Jane was resolved to receive no kindness from *her*." However, she has the consolation of her good intentions and feels sure that George will approve them.

### Commentary

As the novel draws toward its close, some of the plot elements develop rapidly, set free to a degree by the death of Mrs. Churchill. For Emma two opposite relationships develop. While she proves herself to George and comes to more understanding with him, she gets from Jane some comeuppance different from that which came from Augusta Elton; in this instance it comes from someone who, except in the matter of wealth, is Emma's equal but who has not really been treated as an equal by Emma.

*Summary*

One morning ten days after Mrs. Churchill's death, Mr. Weston comes with an urgent request for Emma to come see Mrs. Weston for news about a "most unaccountable business." Emma becomes more and more inquisitive and upset on the way, but for once Mr. Weston will not divulge anything prematurely.

Left alone with an ill-looking Mrs. Weston, Emma learns that Frank has come over to see them that very morning and to break the news that he and Jane Fairfax have been long and secretly engaged—since they were together at Weymouth in October, in fact. Emma is first agitated about her former conversations with Frank about Jane and then in regard to "poor Harriet." She now has to reassure Mrs. Weston that, though briefly it was otherwise, she is not in love with Frank. While Mrs. Weston shows her relief "with tears of joy," Emma states that Frank is greatly to blame for deceiving everyone. After her friend defends him, she speaks out for "upright integrity" and cries out at the indelicacy of letting Jane be "on the point of going as governess." But Frank has known nothing of this until yesterday, after which time he immediately headed for Highbury to see Jane. Mr. Churchill has given his consent to the engagement, and Emma thinks regretfully that he would have done the same for Harriet. When she thinks of Mr. Dixon, she blushes; but in spite of all the upsetting news, she musters her reserves to set Mr. Weston at ease when he re-enters. She does so well, in fact, that on the way home with her Mr. Weston begins to think that the engagement is the best step that Frank could have taken.

*Commentary*

The major portion of this chapter serves to clarify plot elements, but through the surprise and the regrets, Emma is coming to terms more and more with herself and the world she inhabits. She copes admirably with the situation, particularly in regard to Mr. and Mrs. Weston; and the revelation about Frank and Jane is

bound to go beyond her criticism of Frank and the secret engagement to some consideration of deception and scheming in general.
She seems hardly aware, however, of one major development on her
part. Miss Austen has very subtly been enlarging Emma's relationship to George, and at this point in the story Emma criticizes Frank
by describing what she sees as perfection in a man—and does it
apparently without realizing that she is describing George Knightley,
who has earlier indicated what he considers as perfection in a wife.
Basically Emma fits his description too.

Satire is still at work in this chapter. One should note, for instance, what Miss Austen presents about Highbury's reaction to the
death of Mrs. Churchill. Individual satire resides in Emma's still
unresolved relationship with Harriet, a relationship that is very soon
to offer its revelations and comeuppance.

## CHAPTER XI

*Summary*

Still highly concerned about Harriet, Emma decides that "it
was not so much *his* behavior as her *own*" that makes her angry
with Frank. She should have discouraged Harriet's growing attachment and would have, she concludes, if she had had more common
sense. In regard to Jane, she feels relief and wishes her only
happiness.

Harriet arrives and, to Emma's surprise, has learned the news
from Mr. Weston and is quite calm about it. Nonetheless, trying to
cushion what she thinks is a blow, Emma consoles her only to learn
that Harriet's attachment has been, not for Frank, but for George
Knightley. Emma is utterly astounded—so much so that she finally
realizes that "Mr. Knightley must marry no one but herself!" Harriet recounts her reasons for thinking that her feelings are recipro-
cated, and Emma, though she agrees that there may be truth in this,
feels bitter, especially after Harriet says, "But now I seem to feel
that I may deserve him..." Mr. Woodhouse enters and thus stops
the discussion.

After Harriet is gone, Emma is beside herself: "Oh God! that I had never seen her!" She tries to comprehend the situation by first examining her heart, wondering how long George has been so dear to her. She faces up to her own delusions and to ignorance of her own heart. This knowledge of herself reveals her vanity and how "with unpardonable arrogance [she has] proposed to arrange everybody's destiny." Why had she not let Harriet marry Robert Martin? But her pretty friend's "presumption to raise her thoughts to Mr. Knightley" lies at Emma's own door: "Who had been at pains to give Harriet notions of self-consequence but herself?"

*Commentary*

This is the crucial turning point for Emma. She has to acknowledge and try to come to terms with what she has done to Harriet and with the fact that she herself loves George. The situational irony is very strong indeed: Harriet, taught by Emma to look above herself, has looked to the very man who is exactly right for Emma. One could hardly be more fully caught in her own web of scheming. It is never easy to admit that one is wrong, but Emma does it admirably under the circumstances, for her emotions are very strong and are pulled in different directions.

The situation forces Emma to admit that her own imagination was wrong to go against the order of social stratification. Like the other characters, she has believed in it in general; but now the inequality of just one aberration from that order is forcefully impressed upon her. She sees that aberration—her own doing—as wrong and disruptive. She must deal with two misplaced prides—her own and Harriet's newly developed one. Basically what faces her is the necessity of helping or letting the social order reassert itself—if that can be.

## CHAPTER XII

*Summary*

Emma has never known before how much her happiness depends on being first with George. She rationalizes a great deal, deciding that, if she could be sure of his never marrying at all, she would be perfectly satisfied. For Emma feels that she cannot marry because of her father. George is expected back any day, and she can then observe him, but in the meanwhile she resolves against seeing Harriet, an arrangement to which Harriet submits approvingly.

Mrs. Weston calls and recounts her visit that day with Jane, for whom she has nothing but high regard except for the secret engagement. Emma is all sympathy and understanding, very conscious of her past injustice toward Jane. That evening is all gloom for Emma; even the weather adds its share. Hartfield is comparatively deserted and seems likely to become even more so. The child that is to be born will keep the Westons away; Jane and Frank will naturally be leaving; and if George marries Harriet, there will no longer be those friendly and comfortable visits from Donwell Abbey. What increases her wretchedness is the reflection, "never far distant from her mind," that it is all her own work. When she reaches this pitch of thought, she starts, sighs heavily, and walks about the room.

*Commentary*

Emma is experiencing an ultimate degree of comeuppance. Almost everything, including Mrs. Weston's report of Jane, stands in direct contrast to her unhappiness. Emma's reaction to the situation — her feelings and thoughts — epitomize Miss Austen's concern with the results, rather than the high and dramatic moment, of strong emotions. The delineation of Emma's reflections represents the low point of her career, and the question is will she submit to the circumstances or will she find inner resource enough to cope with them, either in the old way or a new one? Is Emma as strong as she has seemed?

**CHAPTER XIII**

*Summary*

The morning's bad weather clears in the afternoon, and Emma goes outdoors for the serenity of the shrubbery. George appears, joins her for the walk, and is silent. Emma finally starts the conversation and learns that he already knows the news about Jane and Frank, was apprised of it only that morning, in fact. When she says that she should have listened to his advice and then sighs, he takes her arm and commiserates with her. Understanding him, she assures him that she was never attached to Frank. He is silent, and she continues by saying that her vanity was flattered by Frank but that she was "somehow or other safe from him." Still George is silent and deep in thought, but finally he says of Frank that "With such a woman he has a chance." Declaring that Frank is a very fortunate man to find such a woman for his wife and at such an early age, George admits that he is envious.

Emma fears that they are within half a sentence of Harriet. She does not encourage him to explain the point of envy, and George takes this in apparent mortification. As they reach the house, she reconsiders his depressed manner and offers to listen as a friend. Shaken, he addresses her as his "dearest Emma" and asks if he has no chance of ever succeeding. She is so utterly agitated by what his words imply that he has to do the talking, and he does quite a convincing job of declaring, in no uncertain terms, his love for her and his wish to hear her speak. "What did she say? — Just what she ought, of course. A lady always does. — She said enough to show there need not be despair — and to invite him to say more himself."

George had certainly not come with the intention of asking her to marry him, but within half an hour he has "passed from a thoroughly distressed state of mind, to something so like perfect happiness, that it could bear no other name." Emma's change is equal. Thus it is that "She was his own Emma, by hand and word, when they returned into the house."

### Commentary

The two preceding chapters have presented and explored an inward change within Emma. The revelations, while leading to the positiveness of self-recognition and self-knowledge, lead also to the negative position involving gloom, despair, estrangement, and isolation. This chapter constitutes an outward change for Emma and thereby effects a reversal of fortune. Starting out with misunderstandings, it concludes with understanding and positive, happy commitment. Containing a highly interesting rearrangement of human relationships, the three chapters together also constitute the major climax of the novel. This rearrangement of relationships is the process of the social order righting itself, but it is also the natural working of equals finding each other. Though some more rearrangement is to come in order to resolve all the forces set in motion in the novel, the ideal correspondence between natural and social order is well on its way to being realized.

## CHAPTERS XIV-XV

### Summary

Emma is in "an exquisite flutter of happiness" as they sit down to tea, Mr. Woodhouse contentedly unaware of "the impending evil" of the engagement. The night is sleepless for her as she considers what must be done about her father and Harriet and decides that, while her father lives, she and George can be only engaged. In determining how least to be Harriet's "enemy," she decides to communicate with her only by letter and to get her an invitation to visit the John Knightleys in London. After she sadly writes the letter early the next morning, George comes for breakfast and has hardly left when a thick letter arrives from Randalls, containing a long explanatory letter from Frank to Mrs. Weston. It is a good and believable letter which, in Emma's present state of mind and heart, mostly exonerates Frank for his past actions in Highbury. Among other explanations, he says that he felt that Emma had guessed the truth about him and Jane and that at the end of his first visit he had almost confessed the truth to her. He also discloses that it was he who sent Jane the pianoforte. He has nothing but good words for Emma. For himself he expresses both justification and regret.

Because of the letter, Emma's former regard for the writer returns and she desires George to read the letter also. As he does, he occasionally makes a comment and concludes by feeling better about Frank. Then he turns to the problem of Mr. Woodhouse. The only way he can see to ask her to marry him without "attacking the happiness of her father" is for himself to come and live at Hartfield. She promises to think it over, and the proposition becomes more and more reasonable as she dwells upon it. But there is still the problem of Harriet, who is hardly likely to find in time that George is less worthy of worship than Mr. Elton was found to be. And it is really "too much to hope even of Harriet, that she could be in love with more than *three* men in one year."

## Commentary

The emphasis in these chapters is upon clearing up matters in regard to Frank, and this is done primarily through his letter and the reaction to it by Emma and George. One sidelight to George's reading the letter is the forecast of what the domestic situation will be for him and Emma: it will obviously be comfortable and lively, a true meeting of minds and hearts with just enough difference thrown in for interesting variety. While an answer is found to the problem of Mr. Woodhouse as an obstacle to marriage, Emma's private problem of Harriet, of whose affection for him George knows nothing, continues. Superb novelist as she is, Miss Austen keeps a suspenseful facet of the plot developing to help support the leisureliness of her exploratory denouement. At the end of Chapter XV there is a faint and almost nostalgic echo of Emma's original willful desire to maneuver someone into marriage when she thinks it is too much to hope Harriet could love three men in one year.

## CHAPTER XVI

### Summary

Harriet proves to be as desirous of avoiding a meeting as is Emma, and Emma has no trouble getting her invited and off to London for at least a fortnight. Wanting to wait until Mrs. Weston is delivered of her baby before telling Mr. Woodhouse of her engagement, Emma now has adequate time and takes the opportunity to call on Jane, who meets her on the stairs herself. She is very gratified by Jane's greeting, then hears Augusta Elton within. Inside, the latter meets Emma with unusual graciousness because she thinks she alone is in on the secret of Jane's engagement and proves her attitude by her constant tasteless asides and "secret" teasings of Jane. Mr. Elton is expected to pick up his wife after (Augusta asserts) a meeting with Mr. Knightley at the Crown, a meeting that Emma says is to be tomorrow. Emma is proved right when Mr. Elton arrives hot and disconcerted after a long walk to Donwell Abbey, where he was unable to find George in spite of having sent a letter. Emma can smile because she guesses that George is waiting for her at Hartfield. When she leaves, Jane attends her all the way downstairs, where they both apologize and forgive each other for their misunderstandings. Emma is happy to learn that Jane and Frank's living with Mr. Churchill at Enscombe is settled, and she concludes thus: "Oh! if you knew how much I love every thing that is decided and open!"

### Commentary

In case there was any doubt, this chapter proves the basically good character and personality of Jane. Augusta gets an incidental and minor degree of comeuppance, perhaps all that her small character merits: littleness deserves littleness. Emma, who can now feel tolerant of even an Augusta, has before her, in the person of Jane, a lovely and radiant example of openness, a quality that she can appreciate more than ever because of her wish to be absolutely open and frank with George.

## CHAPTER XVII

### Summary

Mrs. Weston becomes the mother of a little girl, just what Emma had wished for her. George and Emma hardly ever mention Harriet, and Emma is grieved that she cannot be fully open with him about her pretty friend, who is now to remain with the John Knightleys until they all come down in August. Meanwhile Emma finds a time to tell her father of her engagement. Shocked, he tries to dissuade her from it, but she softens him a little by the time George, as planned, arrives to add his suasive powers. Finally, after Isabella through letters and Mrs. Weston in person join the others to persuade him, Mr. Woodhouse begins to think "that some time or other—in another year or two, perhaps—it might not be so very bad if the marriage did take place."

When the news spreads over Highbury, everyone is surprised, but in general the match is very well approved by everybody except Augusta Elton, who pities "poor Knightley."

## Commentary

Working out further the denouement of her plot, Miss Austen makes good satire of Mr. Woodhouse, the man of gentle selfishness whose only real strength seems to lie in the regard that others have for him. The number of forces needed to persuade him is truly comic and represents the degree of regard for a harmless, whimsical old man who has long outgrown any usefulness. Community satire is registered in the town's reaction to the engagement and is pinpointed in Mr. Weston's inability to keep a secret.

## CHAPTER XVIII

### Summary

The visit of the John Knightleys is drawing close and Emma is dreading meeting Harriet when one morning George comes in with the news that Harriet is going to marry Robert Martin. Emma is amazed and hides her delight with difficulty. Robert has been to London, where, in seeing the Knightleys, he has also seen Harriet and proposed again, this time successfully. George feels that Emma will be against the marriage, but she finally convinces him that she is not, that she now agrees with him about the rightness of a union between Robert and Harriet.

On one of their now daily visits to Randalls, Emma and her father arrive to find Jane and Frank there. Frank asks and receives her pardon for his past actions. He is still a lively person, and Emma suggests that he must have gotten some pleasure out of deceiving everyone formerly. When he denies it, she says, "... to tell you the truth, I think it might have been some amusement to myself in the same situation. I think there is a little likeness between us." Frank jokes about some of the past events, and Jane is forced to smile even as she admonishes him. On the way home, Emma is pleased with seeing Frank, but in comparing him and George she happily finds more worth in the latter.

### Commentary

Emma's final problem is resolved without her assistance: Harriet's natural propensity for being in love rectifies the situation, and in the proper direction. The meeting with Frank at the Westons gets him gracefully off the scene and off Emma's conscience. In leading her to compare the only two men toward whom she has been inclined, the meeting serves to confirm her and the reader in her choice. Miss Austen has succeeded in pairing off each eligible person, including Mr. Elton, with the proper mate.

## CHAPTER XIX

### Summary

The party comes from London, and an hour alone with Harriet proves to Emma that "Robert Martin had thoroughly supplanted Mr. Knightley." Harriet's father is learned to be a well-to-do tradesman, who treats Robert liberally; and in becoming acquainted with Robert, Emma finds him a man of sense and worth.

The first of the three engagements to reach the altar is that of Robert and Harriet in September. In November Jane and Frank are to be married. Emma and George fix upon October, but Mr. Woodhouse cannot be induced to consent. As long as he is unhappy about it, Emma feels that she cannot proceed. Fortunately for the betrothed, Mrs. Weston's poultry house is robbed one night of all its turkeys and other poultry yards suffer the same fate. This is tantamount to housebreaking with Mr. Woodhouse, who feels safe only with the male Knightleys, and John must soon return to London! The result is that, with more cheerful consent from her father than Emma could have hoped, the wedding takes place and all hopes and wishes of friends are "fully answered in the perfect happiness of the union."

*Commentary*

The good-natured satire on marriage is obvious here, containing, as it does, the irony of how unequal events are related. It is noteworthy, however, that before the "happy ending" the standing social order is fully reasserted: the intimacy between Harriet and Emma "must sink; their friendship must change into a calmer sort of good-will; and, fortunately, what ought to be, and must be, seemed already beginning, and in the most gradual, natural manner." The degree to which Emma now accepts this social order is given rather tongue-in-cheek when she learns of Harriet's parentage and reflects upon her possibly being matched with George or Frank or even Mr. Elton: "The stain of illegitimacy, unbleached by nobility or wealth, would have been a stain indeed."

Emma has come a long way to self-recognition and self-knowledge; the social aberration that resulted from her willful imagination, having failed to mature, is safely past; and the social order of the provincial community settles back to normal. Actually, the reader can see, when he looks back at Miss Austen's characterizations and plot structuring, that neither of the three men would have married Harriet any more than Emma would have had Mr. Elton. Consequently, the supreme irony of the story may be that, though a few characters were for a while upset or in doubt about events, there was never any danger at all of the community social order being subverted. Each couple is paired off in the novel in terms of being of similar social rank and in terms of natural equality — even the Eltons. The ending, then, is "happy" as an ideal union of the social and the natural.

# CRITICAL ANALYSIS

The following analyses are meant to be suggestive, not exhaustive. Indeed, they are deliberately far from being complete, for they are intended to give a beginning and point the way. The good critical reader will explore the novel for further detailed confirmation of these analyses. The better critical reader will also find other points of analytic approach and will take reasoned issue with some of the statements made here.

## PLOT

Some generalization should be kept in mind when one considers the plot of *Emma*. Perhaps first should be a reminder of the seeming leisureliness with which Miss Austen puts her story together. Practically none of the material is, in the usual sense, exciting—that is, there is little external climactic action, and there is no adventurous action. Primarily the reasons are that it is a satirical novel about social manners and mores and that the satire comes more from the effects of emotion than from emotion itself. However, the novel will appear leisurely written only on one's first reading. Once the reader knows the outcome of events and repeats the novel, he will find that it is one of the most tightly knit works ever done. For, since much of the book is plotted for purposes of irony (which shows the difference between intention and performance or the difference between what a character knows and what others, including the reader at times, know), the repeating reader can relish the minuteness with which Miss Austen has prepared for and then exploits to the full the misunderstandings and the foibles of the people in her provincial community, especially those of Emma. For instance, all that Frank Churchill does and says on the party to Box Hill takes on the meaning of *double entendre* for the re-reader, who now discovers that it is leisurely only in appearance. Similarly, one can sense the irony in how Emma misconstrues Mr. Elton's gallantry or Harriet's attachment for Mr. Knightley simply because the characters are too mannered to speak directly.

The plot structure of the novel is regulated in part by division into three volumes: in Volume One Emma deceives herself about Mr. Elton and that deception reaches its climax in his declaration in the carriage; Volume Two shows her deceiving herself about Frank Churchill and getting over it in a much less climactic fashion; Volume Three continues her self-deception about people but reaches its major climax in the ultimate revelation about herself and George Knightley. Obviously many other developing facets are involved, but in brief outline these are the three rising and falling stages of action in the novel. Only the last one, however, is final, for Emma throughout is more and more self-deceived, though at the same time she is also moving toward self-knowledge which will let her come to terms with herself and her situation.

This is only the skeletal plot structure, and it is fleshed out in many ways. To comprehend this fleshing out, the reader should remember that the motive force for plot in fiction is generally one or more of three kinds of conflict: man against man, man against environment, or man against himself. The force of man-against-man is incidental but important to the overall satire of the novel and can be seen in the social maneuverings of various characters. The force of man-against-environment is seen primarily in terms of Emma versus her social milieu: she goes against the accepted manners and social ranks in trying to manipulate Harriet either from or into the social and personal lives of others. But the most consistent plot force in the novel is man-against-himself: Emma is constantly deceiving herself and is thus in conflict with herself. All three motive forces for plot, then, are found in *Emma,* but the last two predominate and are in essence the same, for Emma is ironically against herself because she is against her environment. She has accepted the code of her society but at the same time, due to her imbalance of imagination and reason, she wants to go against it; both the code and her opposing willfulness are important to her—hence conflict.

The overall pattern of plot movement is rather classic. Emma's conflict begins when her willful imagination is released by the loss of Miss Taylor; her situation is like a vacuum to be filled—and fulfilled—in accordance with her nature. The result is a continuous rising interest for the reader as Emma's self-deception realizes and manifests itself. The major climax, the highest point of reader interest, comes in Chapters XI, XII, and XIII in the final volume, followed by an unraveling denouement. This movement designed to increase reader interest can be charted like the rising, peaking, and falling on a graph.

Finally, another major plot pattern used in the novel is that of contrast. Plot manipulation not only arranges to juxtapose significantly different characters (Frank and George, for instance) but also often develops a special rhythm by placing introspective scene or chapter next to one of social interaction.

Thus the plot is quite complex, with more than one element often working at once. Composed of classic pattern, contrast, and planned general social satire, all facets are based upon conflict. Though not as obvious as the others, even the last-mentioned element (which is man-against-man) stems from the conflict between social intention and performance. Underlying all of these conflicts is the motive of comic irony.

## SETTING

Austen's setting is that of a provincial community, particularly as it involves the gentry of the region. One is hardly aware of the geography of the locale. The closeness of the town of Highbury and the estates of Hartfield, Donwell Abbey, and Randalls is made clear, as is the fact that London is sixteen miles away; but, except for the description of Donwell (which is shown for the purpose of giving Emma's reaction to it), physical aspects of the country are not dwelt upon. For instance, Harriet meets the gypsies on the Richmond road and is "saved" by Frank; but, other than the fact that there is an embankment over which her original companion scrambles, all we learn is that there is a Richmond road.

Primarily the setting is the drawing room or its equivalent. Even the scene at Box Hill is in essence merely an outdoor drawing room, and so is the shrubbery walk where George proposes to Emma. Vegetation and terrain are barely mentioned if at all, for the real setting is the social involvement, the human relations, which are not connected with the specifics of geography. Instead, they find their natural setting among the drawing rooms, the dining rooms, the rooms for dancing, the carriages, and the paraphernalia of entertainment such as charades and word games.

## POINT OF VIEW

By and large the point of view is that of Emma, a necessary one if Austen is to explore the character of a willful and somewhat snobbish young lady and at the same time keep the reader's sympathy for her. Only thus can we be convinced that Emma's character really blends honesty and goodwill with its negative qualities; it is thus too that we can best view the effects of emotion rather than dwell upon climactic emotion itself.

At times the point of view is that of the author. Though this subject comes also under Style (see below), it should be said here that, in order to get the necessary ironic distance from her characters, the author not only very occasionally gets briefly into the point of view of other characters but also skillfully pulls the reader back to her own point of view in order that he see things in terms of ironic satire. If he is too close, his reader involvement may lead merely to critical disgust. At the proper distance, he is involved only enough to appreciate the comic satire. When necessary for proper distancing, then, Austen simply moves into authorial point of view as, for instance, in the scene where George proposes to Emma: "What did she say?—Just what she ought, of course. A lady always does.—She said enough to show there need not be despair—and to invite him to say more himself." This shift to authorial point of view avoids sentimentality and allows both humor and irony in reference to the coyness and indirection that a consistently social person may give to a vital and personal occasion. And it does all this better than in the details of dialogue, where the point might be lost without brevity.

Point of view, then, is omniscient when it is to the author's purpose (we do not, for instance, get into the points of view of Jane or Frank, for doing so would give away too much), but the character whose point of view is most before us is Emma, the focal personage of the novel.

## CHARACTERS

With the exception of Emma, the characters are generally static ones. They do not change. Rather, they are likely to be simply confirmed in their views, for they live in and accept a stable if static society. Nonetheless, the type of characters portrayed is varied and so is the degree of their realistic development.

Among the lesser developed but important ones, we may note Mr. Woodhouse, John Knightley, and Augusta Elton. They appear to be one-dimensional because they consistently show their one dominant coloring, and so far as treatment of them in the novel is concerned, they are one-dimensional. Mr. Woodhouse, in his gentle selfishness, is the petty arch-conservative, wanting absolutely nothing to change and constantly being apprehensive about matters of health. John is similar but in domestic terms; he is rather unsocial because he wants to rest content with his family in his domestic comforts. Augusta is always seen as the talkative busybody who preens herself on her supposed social importance. They serve their purposes in the novel best by being one-sided, and they come very close to being caricatures.

Miss Bates deserves a bit of special attention. She is like an archetype of the boring non-stop talker. But she takes on added dimension by the very fact that her gush of words encompasses everything around her — so much so, in fact, that the small and the important apparently have equal significance for her. A thwarted woman (though she would never recognize herself as such), she has a driving need to express herself, though her expression is never egocentric. She is, indeed, one of the most kindhearted and thankful persons imaginable; but she is also capable of being hurt and of forgiving. She undergoes no observable change in the novel, but hers is possibly the most fully rounded characterization among the minor ones.

Though one of the more important characters, Harriet Smith is mostly a counter to be moved about by Emma and the plot of the novel. She is a simple but pretty girl who, once in love, will always be in love and who evinces one very interesting though momentary development when she decides that she is after all perhaps worthy of George Knightley.

Jane Fairfax is a skillfully employed foil for Emma, but we do not get to know her in dramatic detail because she is involved in a mystery and much about her must remain unknown until it is revealed in summary. On the other hand, Frank Churchill, though he too is involved in the mystery, comes through with better delineation. He has admirable abilities but is too frivolous to be truly admirable; his mainstay is social charm and wit. He is important partly because in many respects he is the male counterpart of Emma: both get a certain enjoyment out of seeing others labor under misapprehensions, and it is significant that Emma recognizes this lively similarity near the end of the story.

George Knightley is one of the most important figures in the book, though during much of the time he is rather in the background of events. He is a man of benevolence. He is the only one strong enough to impress Emma with critical good sense, and he is thus the only logical one that she can marry. He is particularly significant to the novel, however, because he is the *raisonneur,* the spokesman character for Miss Austen. His reasoning and comment upon events are pretty much those of the author, and he constitutes a rational thread of cohesiveness running through the novel.

Emma Woodhouse is the main character and hers is the most fully rounded, three-dimensional characterization. Her dominant trait is willful imagination, but she also has the elements of goodwill, rationality, and proportion when her willfulness does not lead her into self-deception. She is the fundamental changing character in the book, for she goes through a slow and bumpy growth from self-deception to self-knowledge. She is the book's aberration from the static social norm, and at the end she has developed to the point of fitting properly into her social milieu. Her characterization has been so well done that one cannot be absolutely sure that she will never scheme again, but one can feel that she has a good chance of remaining on terms with herself and her environment because of her growth and because she now has George Knightley beside her.

In considering the characters of the book, one should remind himself that, no matter how well they are developed for their individuality, they also serve for purposes of satirical contrast and comparison. The distancing that Austen achieves through point of view (see above) effects a kind of balance between the individual as such and his place in a satirically social context.

## THEME

The theme is man's absurdities—not the high-minded and exceptional absurdities of tragedy or the grim ones of Swiftean satire, but those common, frequent, and more laughable ones of society, its code of manners, and its fabricated engagement of man's time, thought, and energy.

Beneath Austen's satiric comedy is a moralistic realism. By picturing the real incongruities of social matters, she implies what may be right: the ideal balance between head and heart, between common sense and goodness, between rationality and imagination or emotion. Hers is not a naturalistic world inimical to or destructive of the individual. Rather, it is a fairly stable social world that operates comfortably as long as there is no major aberration from it. It can, in fact (if we judge from the outcome of the story), operate effectively in spite of an aberration, secure that the deviation can be recitified and absorbed so that the deviant (Emma) finds and accepts her proper place.

It is against this background that Emma pursues her willful and subsequently crossed-purpose way. In the end her change is not into something new and different from her time and place, but into something that is the standard of her environment. Her change is not the kind associated with a liberal idea of progress, but the kind found in the conservative idea of progress: she develops into, not out of, a social tradition. Thus a major thematic irony of the book is that at the end Austen lets the reader see that, in spite of the surface doubts and disturbance, there was never any real danger that the environmental fabric would be changed because of, or for, Emma. This certainty is driven home by the comfortable (and, literarily, conventional) pairing off of the marriageable couples.

Nevertheless, the triumph of this social world does not mean that it is necessarily the best of its kind. Thematic satire at the expense of the manners and people of this world is given throughout the book. A crowning irony comes at the very end when Emma and George can be comfortably paired off in marriage only because the robbing of poultry houses makes Mr. Woodhouse want George around for protection. Such a relationship between cause and effect—between the ludicrous and the desirable—underscores the inclusive satirical theme of incongruity. By moralistic implication a world of balanced congruities is yet to be attained.

## STYLE

Perhaps the best description of style in *Emma* is that it is quietly subtle. The tone of the book is one of absolute ease and surety on the part of the author, who handles her material with such deft touches that an unperceptive reader may conclude that the story and the writing are very ordinary. But Austen's method is nearer that of the magician than that of the boxer.

She can be disarmingly simple and direct as, for instance, she sets up Emma's situation at the very beginning of the book; but she is also carefully and unobtrusively setting up objects of satire when she refers to Emma's always doing just as she liked or to Mr. Woodhouse's having been a valetudinarian all his life. When she describes Mr. Elton as "a young man living alone without liking it," she pins down a character specimen as neatly intact as can be done. The wit and sharp edge of her phrasing are illustrated when she describes Isabella's Christmas visit with her father and sister: "It was a delightful visit; — perfect, in being much too short." She also makes use of the subtle antithetic balance of word and phrasing derived from the eighteenth-century literary stylists: when Frank Churchill's visit is again postponed, Mrs. Weston, "after all her concern for what her husband was to suffer, suffered a great deal more herself." Although she avoids figurative images, Austen is adept at coining pregnant abstractions in the manner of Dr. Samuel Johnson: note the "apparatus of happiness" placed in the dialogue of Mrs. Elton.

In general, her style achieves exactly the proper distancing she wants between the reader and the fictional subject (see above under Point of View), and the reader is affected whether he is aware of it or not. To do this she may withdraw herself (and the reader with her) somewhat from the immediate subject by using a euphemistic circumlocution that contains an ironic barb. For instance, in reference to Mr. Elton's marriage and Harriet's feelings for him, Emma's thoughts are stated with third-person indirectness as "It was not to be doubted that poor Harriet's attachment had been an offering to conjugal unreserve"; to grasp the irony one may note the connotations of the world *offering,* while to comprehend the distancing of phraseology he may compare a direct statement like "At some intimate moment he told his wife of Harriet." A major difference is that Austen's phrasing disengages us just enough to let us laugh at what is, after all, a natural process of married communication.

Another way of stylistic distancing is the use of anticlimax. When Emma and George have become engaged and return to the house, Mr. Woodhouse is anxious that George not take a cold from his earlier ride; the author's wry comment is that "Could he have seen the heart, he would have cared very little for the lungs." Anticlimax can also be brutally though subtly frank in observations on mankind. The authorial statement about the death of Mrs. Churchill is this: "It was felt as such things must be felt. Everybody had a degree of gravity and sorrow; tenderness towards the departed, solicitude for the surviving friends; and, in a reasonable time, curiosity to know where she would be buried." This is an acute and realistic observation, but the concluding anticlimax ironically points to the difference between human intention and performance. Immediately following this observation is a stylistic illustration of the influence from the eighteenth-century concern for balancing phrasing and the eighteenth-century penchant for epigram: "Goldsmith tells us, that when lovely woman stoops to folly, she has nothing to do but to die; and when she stoops to be disagreeable, it is equally to be recommended as a clearer of ill-fame." Only through stylistic treatment such as this could Austen have provided for the reader the necessary esthetic distance to appreciate the latent satire connected with a serious subject like death.

Finally, in discussing Austen's style, one has to point to what has been called her mastery of dialogue. Her ear for the way women in particular talk is very good indeed. And though Augusta Elton's attempts at cleverness make a fine example, the best is Miss Bates's fragmentary speech, her habitual tone. But in terms of authorial style, it should be further noted that the use of direct and indirect conversation varies according to how much the reader needs to be involved in the immediate material, for the indirect reportage puts more distance between the reader and the material and allows at times a better satirical view.

Thus, from the smallest choice of words to the largest presentation of conversations and scenes, Austen's style is subtle and may be witty, sharp, epigrammatic, abstract, or distancing according to the satiric need.

# QUESTIONS FOR STUDY AND REVIEW

1. Is *Emma* a unified novel? If so, where does the unity lie — in the plot, the characters, the setting, the theme, the style, the mood?

2. How does the fact that Jane Austen stretches out her climaxes relate to her concentrating her interest on exploring the effects of emotion rather than on the critical high moments of emotion?

3. Look up the term *sentimental novel* and determine whether any major elements of that form are used in *Emma*.

4. Describe the plot structure of the novel. Is only one structure involved?

5. Explain the ways in which Jane Austen uses contrast to effect irony. Are the contrasts simple and clear-cut?

6. Are there any general contrasts such as the difference between generations?

7. What evidence from this novel can you give for or against the critical statement that Jane Austen's point of view is a feminine one?

8. Many have noted that Miss Austen's novels lack any large historical perspective and lack making use of historical events of the day. Can you defend these lacks in *Emma?*

9. Critics have remarked that the character Emma refuses to let herself be basically involved with or committed to fundamental human concerns. On what levels can you either defend or refute this criticism?

10. In what ways is the setting important to the theme of the novel?

11. Describe the character of Miss Bates and point to instances in which she is important for the satirical delineation of manners.

12. Compare and contrast Miss Bates and Augusta Elton as two compulsive talkers.

13. Who is the *raisonneur* in the novel and what is his purpose?

14. Re-examine man's absurdities as they are treated in this novel. Are they absurd because they are exceptional? Why or why not?

15. In what ways is *Emma* a realistic novel, or is it not realistic at all? Justify your answer.

16. What would you say is the largest and most controlling ironic treatment in the novel? Is the reader aware of it most of the time?

17. Enumerate ways in which the eighteenth-century attitude toward social ranks is exemplified in the novel.

18. What are some elements of literary style that Miss Austen inherited from the eighteenth century?

19. What is meant by *esthetic distance?* How is it achieved in *Emma?*

20. Why do you suppose Miss Austen, who could liken her literary work to a little bit of ivory, avoids figurative imagery in *Emma?* Is this avoidance related to esthetic distance?

21. It is often stated that good literature bears re-reading. In what ways is this particularly true of *Emma?*

22. Consider in order the instances when Emma arrives at some degree of self-knowledge. Can you relate these instances to the plot pattern?

23. What characters other than Emma show an awareness of self-importance? How do they function thematically in relation to Emma?

24. Miss Austen has been accused of cold detachment from her fictional subject matter. What reasons can you give for this accusation? Can a satirist be thoroughly detached from what he is writing about?

25. Why do you suppose Miss Austen once said that Emma is "a heroine whom no one but myself will much like"? Is a liking of subject matter necessary for proper appreciation of a work of art? Is something else equally or more important?

## SELECTED BIBLIOGRAPHY

Allen, Walter. *The English Novel: A Short Critical History.* New York, 1958. A study that "places" Jane Austen in the history of English fiction.

Booth, Wayne C. "Point of View and the Control of Distance in *Emma,*" *Nineteenth Century Fiction,* XVI (September, 1961), 95-116. A perceptive essay on the rhetoric in *Emma.*

Cecil, Lord David. *Jane Austen.* Cambridge, 1935. A study of the subject matter of Austen's novels, originally the Leslie Stephen Lecture delivered at the University of Cambridge.

Chapman, R. W. *Jane Austen: Facts and Problems.* Oxford, 1948. Piecemeal but suggestive biographical details done by Jane Austen's modern editor, originally the Clark Lectures given at the University of Cambridge.

Hughes, R. E. "The Education of Emma Woodhouse," *Nineteenth-Century Fiction,* XVI (June, 1961), 69-74. A study of Emma's "education" in regard to love and wealth.

Lascelles, Mary. *Jane Austen and Her Art.* London, 1939. A wide-ranging study that combines biography with detailed examination of the novelist's style and general narrative art.

Mudrick, Marvin. *Jane Austen: Irony as Defense and Discovery.* Princeton, 1952. A provocative "new view" of the novels which are examined in individual critical chapters.

Warner, Sylvia Townsend. *Jane Austen: 1771-1817.* London, 1951. A study of the novels as they relate to Jane Austen's biography, with emphasis on the latter.

# NOTES